The Making of the United Kingdom

1500 - 1750

J F AYLETT

Hodder & Stoughton

A MEMBER OF THE HODDER HEADLINE GROUP

ACKNOWLEDGEMENTS

The cover illustration is 'The Coming of the Storm' by David Teniers.

The Publishers would like to thank the following for permission to reproduce copyright illustrations: Breamore House, Nr. Fordingbridge, Hants cover. The Bridgeman Art Library p.4 left; p.7; p.16; p.23 right; p.31; p.34 right; p.36 left; p.48 right; p.51 left; p.55 left. Reproduced by Permission of the Dean and Canons of Windsor p.5 left. By Courtesy of The National Portrait Gallery, London p.5 right; p.24 left; p.33; p.42 left; 43. Christopher Ridley p.9 left; p.37 left. Batsford p.10 left. Windsor Castle, Royal Library c. 1992 Her Majesty The Queen p. 10 right. The Master and Fellows of Trinity College, Cambridge p.11 right. Courtesy of the Marquess of Salisbury p.12 left; p.13; p.15 lower. Reproduced by Permission of the Viscount de L'Isle, from his private collection. p.14. Reproduced by kind permission of the Geffrye Museum Trust p.16 right. David Robson, Salisbury p.17. Janet and Colin Bord p.18 left. Lauros-Giraudon, Paris p.4 right; Giraudon, Paris p.18 lower left; p.54 right. Fitzwilliam Museum, Cambridge p.19. English Life Publications Ltd p.20 top left. The Librarian, Glasgow University Library p.22 left. The Mansell Collection p.22 top right; p.24 right; p.25; p.44 left; p.45 top; p.53 lower left; By permission of the British Library p.23 lower. From the Collection of His Grace The Duke of Atholl, Blair Castle, Perthshire p.26 left. Stan Peachey p.26 right. The National Maritime Museum, London p.28 left; p.29 right; p.30 left; p.30 right. 'Queen Elizabeth – The Defeat of the Spanish Armada' – St Faith's Church, Gaywood, King's Lynn p.29 left. John Birdsall Photography p.32 left. Trustees of the National Library of Scotland p.34 left. Hulton Picture Company p.35 right; p.36 right; p.40 top left National Portrait Gallery p.40 lower left Historic Royal Palaces p.37 right. Mick Parker/The Sealed Knot p.38 right. Wayland Publishers p.47 right. East Harling Church, Norfolk p.41 right. By Courtesy of the Board of Trustees of the Victoria & Albert Museum p.42 right. The Museum of London p.45 left middle and bottom. Society of Antiquaries of London p.46 left. The J. Allan Cash Photolibrary p.46 right. Paul Draper/Sunday Times, London p.47 top. Edward Dimbylow p.47 lower. Magnum Photos Ltd p.48 left. Bibliotheque Nationale, Paris, p.50 right "By permission of the Admiral President, Royal Naval College, Greenwich and the Director of the Greenwich Hospital" p.52 left. Guildhall Library, City of London p.52 right; p.53 right. Weidenfeld and Nicolson Ltd p.53 upper. Rijksmuseum, Amsterdam p.54 left. The National Library of Wales p.58 left. Camera Press p.56 right. The National Trust p.60 upper left. The Salisbury and South Wiltshire Museum p.61 left. Allsport p.61 upper right. Andrew Steven, Belfast p.61 lower right, Jean Guy/Jules/ANA Press Paris p.63 upper left. Zefa p.63 lower left.

The Publishers would also like to thank the following for permission to reproduce material in this volume: Longman Group UK for the extract from *The Early Modern Age* by L. E. Snellgrove (1972); Thames Television International Limited for the extract from *London, The Making of a City* (1976).

Every effort has been made to trace and acknowledge ownership of copyright. The Publishers will be glad to make suitable arrangements with any copyright holders whom it has not been possible to contact.

British Library Cataloguing in Publication Data
Aylett, J.F.
  The making of the United Kingdom 1500–1750.
  – (Past historic)
  I. Title   II. Series
  941.05

ISBN 0 340 54828 2

First published 1992
Impression No. 10 9 8 7 6 5
Year   1999 1998 1997

© 1992 J. F. Aylett

Illustrations by Philip Page

All rights reserved. No part of this publication may be reproduced or transmitted in any form or by any means, electronic or mechanical, including photocopy, recording, or any information storage and retrieval system, without permission in writing from the publisher or under licence from the Copyright Licensing Agency Limited. Further details of such licences (for reprographic reproduction) may be obtained from the Copyright Licensing Agency Limited, of 90 Tottenham Court Road, London W1P 9HE.

Typeset by Litho Link Limited, Welshpool, Powys, Wales.
Printed in Hong Kong for Hodder & Stoughton Educational, a division of Hodder Headline Plc, 338 Euston Road, London NW1 3BH by Colorcraft Ltd.

This book is dedicated to the first Duke of Bolton who did not speak until late in the day when he considered the air to be purer.

Source D on page 21 is adapted from J Webb (ed.): *Poor Relief in Elizabethan Ipswich* (Suffolk Records Society, IX, 1966) p122-3. Source G on page 45 is taken from: *London – the making of a city* (Thames TV & Modus Operandi Ltd, 1976).

Author's notes
There were two calendars in use after 1582. Catholic countries used the Gregorian calendar which Britain did not adopt until 1752. There was a difference of ten days. This explains why dates of events given here (for instance, of events such as the Armada) may vary from those in other books.

From 1500 to 1750 there were 12 pennies in a shilling and 20 shillings in a pound. One shilling was the equivalent of 5p.

CONTENTS

1 Henry VIII and the Church	4
2 Henry's Children and the Church	8
3 Tudor Monarchs and Parliaments	10
4 Elizabeth and her People	12
5 More Religious Problems	26
6 The Armada: A Great Victory . . . ?	28
7 King James and the Gunpowder Plot	32
8 King and Parliament Disagree	34
9 Towards Civil War	36
10 Civil War and After	38
11 Charles II, the Merry Monarch	42
12 Christopher Wren	46
13 Science	48
14 Superstition and Witchcraft	50
15 1688: Revolution	52
16 Parliament in Control	54
17 Ireland	56
18 A United Kingdom . . .	58
19 Change and Continuity	62
Glossary	64
Index	65

In the 11th century, you may remember, a monk tried to fly. He tied wings to his hands and feet and jumped off the abbey tower. When he broke both his legs, he put his failure down to not wearing a tail.

In 1507, John Damien, an Italian, thought he had solved the problem. The Bishop of Ross described what happened in a book of Scottish history which he wrote in 1570. (It helps to read this with a Scottish accent!)

'He causit maik ane pair of wingis of fedderis, [which] beand fassinit upon him, he flew off the castel wall of Striveling, bot shortlie he fell to the grund and braik his thie-bane.'

Damien knew at once what was wrong. They had put some hen feathers in the wings.

We know about events like this because people took the trouble to record them. By reading them, we can try to understand past centuries and our ancestors who lived in them. Hopefully, this book will help you in the search for that knowledge.

Highlighted words, such as ancestor, are explained in the glossary on page 64.

HENRY VIII AND THE CHURCH

A Catherine of Aragon, as a young woman.

Henry VIII was only 17 years old when he became king in 1509. He was a typical prince of his time. He hunted and wrestled; he was a good tennis-player and famous for jousting . He wrote music and poetry and spoke four languages.

He was also very religious. Like all his citizens, he was Roman Catholic. Three times every day, he attended the service of mass. He even wrote a book supporting the Pope , who was Head of the Catholic Church. In return, the Pope gave him the title *Fidei Defensor*. It means *Defender of the Faith*. You can still see the letters FD on some British coins today.

Henry's father had wanted him to marry Princess Catherine of Aragon. She had already been married to his brother Arthur, who had died. She was six years older than Henry, but he loved his Spanish wife.

They had several children; the only one to live was a girl called Mary. As Catherine grew older, Henry became worried. He believed that a country could only be strong and safe if it was ruled by a king. So he was anxious to have a son.

By 1527, Henry had been attracted to a lady of the court, called Anne Boleyn. She was just 20, half the age of Queen Catherine. She refused to have an affair with Henry; it was marriage or nothing. Henry could have had his pick of other mistresses but he was in love with Anne.

However, marriage to Anne was a problem. The Roman Catholic Church did not approve of divorce. The only way to get one was to get the Pope's special permission. There was little hope of that. The Pope was under the control of the Emperor Charles V. And Charles was Catherine's nephew.

Not surprisingly, the Pope said 'No'. Henry was furious. The king's chief minister, Thomas Wolsey, also tried to persuade the Pope. When he failed, Henry banned Wolsey from his court.

The king's new adviser was Thomas Cromwell. He advised Henry that the English Church should break away from the Roman Catholic Church. Instead of the Pope ruling the English Church, Henry should do it himself.

B Anne Boleyn. Catholics said she was a witch in league with the devil.

C Henry VIII at prayer. This picture comes from the Black Book of the Order of the Garter.

D The Bible: Book of Leviticus, 20:21. Henry thought this verse proved that his marriage to Catherine was wrong.

> If a man marries his brother's wife, they will die childless. He has done [an] unclean thing and has disgraced his brother.

E Catherine of Aragon, painted in later life.

Henry liked the idea. In order to do this, he needed the support of the leading people in the land. In particular, he needed the support of the English Church itself. So he called a Parliament to get them to agree.

Parliament supported Henry against the Pope. So did Thomas Cranmer, the Archbishop of Canterbury. Cranmer announced that Henry's marriage to Catherine had not been legal in the first place. So they were divorced – and Henry married Anne Boleyn in 1533. Their child was a girl: Elizabeth.

In the following year, Parliament made Henry Head of the Church. This meant that the Pope no longer had power over the English Church. From 1538, in every church the Bible was read in English, rather than Latin. At last, people could understand what their religion was teaching them.

Yet Henry made few other changes. Many people, including the king himself, still thought they belonged to the Catholic Church. Some still believed the Pope was their real leader. In time, people began calling them *Roman* Catholics because Rome was where the Pope lived.

> Events usually have more than one cause. The English Church broke from the Roman Catholic Church because Henry wanted a son. But there were other reasons as well. For instance, Emperor Charles V did not want Henry to divorce his aunt.

1. Answer these questions in sentences:
   a) What religion was Henry VIII?
   b) Who was the Pope?
   c) Why did Henry want a son?
   d) Look at any coins you have with you. Which ones have the letters *FD* on them?

2. a) Look at the following possible causes for the break from the Roman Catholic Church. Give each one a mark out of ten to show how important you think it was:
   (i) Henry wanted a son;
   (ii) The Pope did not want to give Henry a divorce;
   (iii) Henry loved Anne Boleyn;
   (iv) Catherine was too old to have more children;
   (v) Emperor Charles did not want Henry to divorce Catherine;
   (vi) Henry thought Princess Mary would not make a good queen.
   b) Look at the one which you gave the highest mark. Why do you think this was the main cause of the break?

3. a) Compare sources A and E. How has Catherine changed?
   b) Does this comparison suggest another reason why Henry wanted a divorce? Explain your answer very carefully.

THE END OF THE MONASTERIES

Henry VIII enjoyed wearing fine clothes and precious jewels. He also believed that kings should win honour in war. All this was expensive. As the years passed, Henry found money running out.

However, now he was head of a Church which was very rich. And the richest of all Church properties were the monasteries and nunneries. They owned one quarter of all the land in England; their income was even greater than Henry's. It is easy to see how tempting Henry found them.

So Henry gave orders for officials to examine all the smaller monasteries and nunneries. These had an income of less than £200 a year. There was no need, he said, to look at the bigger ones; they were doing a good job.

In January 1535, these officials set out to find out about the morals of the monks and nuns. In other words, were they being as good as they were supposed to be? As a check, they asked local people, too. They visited 800 monasteries and nunneries in just six months. Considering how bad the roads were, it was quite an achievement.

The questions were not really very important. There were nearly 10,000 monks and nuns in England and Wales. No one really expected that every single one led a holy life.

For instance, monks and nuns promised to stay poor. But, during the middle ages, some monasteries and nunneries had become very rich. It was too easy to prove that this vow was not being kept.

In any case, the officials knew what sort of evidence Henry wanted. Their reports included plenty of juicy scandal. It is hard to tell how much of it was made up.

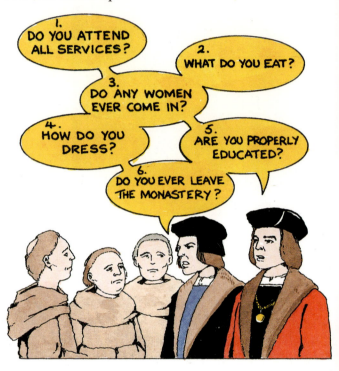

Some of the questions asked.

A This is part of just one report – on Bury St Edmunds.
> The abbot delighted in playing dice and spent much money on it, and in building for his pleasure. He did not preach openly.
>
> Concerning the convent, we could get little or no reports among them. Yet it is proved that there was a frequent coming and going of women to the monastery. Among the relics we found the coals that St Laurence was toasted with, the [cuttings] of St Edmund's nails, and different skulls for the headache.

It was just the sort of evidence that Henry needed. In 1536, an Act of Parliament closed down all the smaller monasteries and nunneries. Over the next four years, the larger ones were also shut. Remember that these were the ones which had been doing a good job as recently as 1534! All their property went straight to Henry VIII.

Very few abbots opposed the king; a handful who did were hanged. Most monks and nuns went quietly. So did the 3000 friars, whose buildings were also closed. The monks were given pensions and many became parish priests.

B This 19th-century painting shows Syon Nunnery being closed by royal officials.

The nuns were less lucky. They were not allowed to marry. Nor, of course, could they become priests. Some received just a gown from the king with which to start their new life. Some of the servants ended up as farm labourers; others were reduced to begging.

Henry had a different end in view for one former archbishop. He declared that St Thomas Becket was not really a saint at all. So his body was dug up and the bones were burned. There were protests throughout Europe. People were horrified.

Henry intended to keep the lands and rent them out. But more wars, against France and Scotland, meant that he needed money fast. So he sold most of the land to nobles and other rich gentlemen. When he died in 1547, Henry had very little left of the monasteries' great wealth.

C What Henry gained from the closures (1536-8). These figures are from official accounts. (A craftsman's annual wage at this time was £3.)

Income:	£
From receivers of purchased land	27,732
From sale of gold and silver plate	6,987
From various fines	5,948
From sale of lands	29,847
From fines for leases	1,006
From other sources	95
Total receipts	71,617
Less:	
Expenses, pensions, etc	12,701
Errors and accounting costs	60
Total deductions	12,762
Profit	58,855

1. a) For each source, write down whether it is primary or secondary.
   b) Look carefully at the secondary source. What would the person who made this have needed to know?
2. a) What two reasons are given for closing the monasteries?
   b) Which was Henry's real reason? Explain how you decided.
   c) Why do you think Henry was so keen to prove that monks and nuns were not keeping their vows?
   d) Look at the questions asked. Write down one answer to each question which would prove that the monks were not living properly.
3. In source A, in what three ways was the abbot doing wrong?
   b) What were the nuns doing wrong?
   c) How could this have been 'proved'?
4. Look at source B and think carefully.
   a) What good were gold *objects* to Henry?
   b) What might Henry do with stained glass windows?
   c) What else in the picture is worth money to Henry?

2 HENRY'S CHILDREN AND THE CHURCH

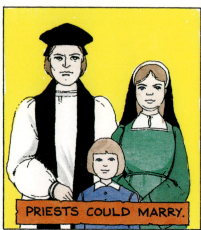

Henry VIII had four more wives after Anne Boleyn but only one more child. It was a boy and they called him Edward. When a British monarch dies, the eldest son always becomes the new ruler. So, Henry's son, Edward, became the next king.

Henry had made few changes to the Church but one of them was very important. The monarch was now in charge of it. That meant Edward could change the Church in any way he wished.

Edward was just nine years old when he became king. He was a weak and sickly child who died just six years later. He was too young to run the country. For most of his reign, his uncle, the Duke of Somerset, took charge.

Yet Edward believed deeply in the Protestant faith. The Duke could not have made the changes he did without the young king's agreement. You can see the changes made in his reign in the pictures above.

At that time, the Church was very important in people's lives. Pictures of hell showed them what happened if they did not lead a good life. No wonder people had strong views about how to pray and worship. They believed that only the right way could take them to heaven.

There were bound to be people who did not like the changes. Londoners complained that the new prayer book did not go far enough: it was too like the old one. In the west country, people did not like saying prayers in English. It was like a foreign language to them. (So was Latin, of course, but they were used to that.)

A *The Chronicle of the Greyfriars of London* described changes made in 1547. This is the original spelling. It may help to read it aloud. Alle imagys pullyd downe thorrow alle Ynglonde att that tyme, and alle churches new whytte-lymed, with the commandmenttes wryttyne on the walles. The 16th day of November at nyghte was pullyd downe the Rode in Powlles with Mary and John, with all the images in the churche. Too of the men that labord at yt was slayne and [various] other sore hurtte.

In 1553, Edward's half-sister Mary became queen. Her mother was Catherine of Aragon; Mary had been brought up as a Catholic. She soon married King Philip of Spain, another Roman Catholic. (His father had been Emperor Charles, who had supported Queen Catherine against Henry.)

Queen Mary was determined to make her people Catholic once more. The Pope took over again as Head of the Church. Inside the churches themselves, the statues returned; so did the priests' brightly-coloured robes. The services they led were said in Latin. Married priests had to leave their wives or give up their jobs.

Some Protestants refused and were burned to death. It was, Mary thought, the best way of getting rid of their sin – the sin of being Protestant. The Protestants saw it differently. They nicknamed the queen 'Bloody Mary'.

E The Pope (left), with a Cardinal (right). The words mean (left) 'An evil church has the face of a devil' and (right) 'Sometimes wise men, sometimes foolish.'

The poem mentions Henry's other daughter, Elizabeth. When Mary died in 1558, Elizabeth became queen. She made the Church Protestant once more but she did not want more deaths and burnings. She wanted to bring peace to her land.

She made herself 'Governor of the Church'. It was a clever title. Catholics could still believe, if they wished, that the Pope was the Church's real leader. The English prayer book was brought back. And priests were allowed to get married.

By and large, people accepted these changes, although some Catholics followed their own religion in private. However, people still argued about religion.

B Queen Mary blessing rings which were supposed to cure sickness (a 16th-century picture).

C John Foxe, a Protestant minister, included these figures in his *Book of Martyrs* (1563), after Mary's death. A martyr is someone who dies for what they believe in.

The whole number burned during the reign of Mary amounted to 284. There were burnt 5 bishops, 21 ministers, 8 gentlemen, 84 workers, 100 farmers, servants and labourers, 26 wives, 20 widows, 9 girls, 2 boys, 2 infants.

D This old East Anglian rhyme shows how ordinary people felt about the burnings.

When William Allen at Walsingham
For trueth was tried in fiery flame;
When Roger Cooe, that good olde man,
Did lose his lyfe for Christe's name;
When these with other were put to death,
We wishte for our Elizabeth.

> Propaganda is an attempt to get other people to believe what you believe. Protestants wanted people to believe that the Protestant religion was the true religion. Catholics wanted people to believe that Protestants were wicked.

1. a) Look at the changes made by Edward VI. Which ones do you think would not have mattered to ordinary people? Give reasons.
   b) Which ones do you think would most have annoyed Catholics? Again, give reasons.
   c) Look carefully at source B. How can you tell that Mary was a Catholic?
   d) Was the writer of source D Catholic or Protestant? Explain how you decided.
2. a) Look at source E and turn the page upside down. What is the artist trying to say about the Pope?
   b) Was this drawn by a Catholic or Protestant? Explain how you decided.
3. a) Think carefully. Which of the sources do you think are propaganda? Give reasons.
   b) Read source A. Suppose you were a journalist. Write about the event for a *Catholic* newspaper.
   c) Now, make up a suitable headline for source A if it were printed in a *Protestant* paper.

3 TUDOR MONARCHS AND PARLIAMENTS

Today, Britain is governed by Parliament. It makes the laws which we all have to obey. Parliament was not so important in the 16th century. Years could pass when it never met at all.

Instead, most decisions were made by the monarch or the chief ministers. These ministers were not elected. The king or queen picked whoever they wanted. Elizabeth often gave jobs to her relatives.

The monarch's chief ministers met in the council. During Elizabeth's reign, there were on average just 13 men in the council, making decisions which affected 4 million people. Generally, the council did what the king or queen wanted it to do.

This council did just about everything which our Parliament does today. It made sure that laws were working; it kept an eye on the law courts. It sent out troops and told the navy when to set sail. It even helped to run the Church.

The council also dealt with many court cases. If necessary, it ordered gaolers to torture people accused of crimes. And all this it did in secret. That is why people in the 16th century began calling it the Privy Council.

B A contemporary picture of Henry VIII opening Parliament in 1523.

A The council could order people to be tortured to make them confess. The prisoner might be hung on a hook or have heavy weights put on his chest. A minister (on the right) was in charge.

Yet there were times when a king or queen needed to call a Parliament. In the 16th century, if monarchs went to war, they had to pay for it themselves. They could get extra money from taxes but Parliament had to agree to these. During his reign, Henry VIII spent a fortune. As a result, the monarchs who came after him needed to call Parliament to get money.

In fact, Tudor monarchs usually only called a Parliament to agree with what they wanted. But this gave members a chance to say what they wanted, too. They expected to be allowed to make their view known.

Even so, Queen Elizabeth still made the decisions. For instance, she did not like Parliament discussing whether she should get married. As soon as she became queen, Parliament wanted her to marry. She refused – and she never did marry.

In fact, she did not use Parliament as much as Henry VIII had done. She reigned for 45 years. Yet Parliament met, altogether, for fewer than three of them. She tried not to spend too much money. That way, she did not have to call Parliament to give her any extra.

Even so, she needed Parliament to meet from time to time. Whenever it did, its members complained about her policies. They went on doing so up to her death.

C Henry VIII on his way to open Parliament in 1512. With him are the great lords who were his chief advisers. The artist had not seen Henry VIII so he drew his father's face instead.

D Elizabeth I speaking to Parliament in about 1601. They called it her 'Golden Speech'.

God hath raised me high [but] I have reigned with your loves. I never was any greedy, scraping grasper, nor yet a waster. My heart was never set upon any worldly goods, but only for my subjects' good. And though you have had and may have many mightier and wiser princes sitting in this seat, yet you never had, nor shall have, any that will love you better.

Historians have to study all sources to decide if they are reliable. There was no shorthand record of what was said in Parliament at this time. Queen Elizabeth's speeches were usually written down from memory.

The queen usually got her own way, although there were times when she gave in gracefully. In 1601, Parliament was complaining about her habit of allowing people the sole right to make or sell something, such as playing-cards. They thought it pushed up prices.

Elizabeth sent a message to Parliament. She said she would stop this at once, if it caused harm. It was a typically clever decision.

Elizabeth kept her Parliaments under control by charm and intelligence. Members knew she loved her country above everything else. But they were restless. There was a growing feeling that monarchs were only human after all. And human beings can make mistakes. The kings who came after her had quite different ideas about their powers.

1 Explain the meaning of (a) Privy Council and (b) Parliament.
2 You need to watch a short video of the State Opening of Parliament to answer this question.
a) How does the scene you see differ from source B?
b) In what ways is the scene similar?
c) Do you think the video is more reliable as evidence than source B? Explain your answer.
3 a) Look at source A. How reliable would this prisoner's confession be? Give reasons.
b) Why do you think monarchs went to such lengths to get a confession?
4 a) Was source C drawn by an eye-witness? Explain how you know.
b) How could a historian check whether this source is reliable? (Give at least two answers.)
5 a) Why is the queen's speech clever?
b) Read the box below source D. What would you want to know about the person who wrote down this speech?

4 ELIZABETH AND HER PEOPLE

A The 'Rainbow Portrait' of Queen Elizabeth I, painted in about 1600. Its symbols show how Elizabeth wanted her people to think of her.

(rainbow = peace)
(serpent = wisdom)
(Elizabeth was the 'eyes and ears' of her country)

Queen Mary died in 1558. Her sister Elizabeth now became the last of Henry's children to rule England and Wales. At one point, Mary had put Elizabeth in the Tower of London. Elizabeth had learned to be cautious.

The new queen had her mother's liveliness and her father's charm. From both of them she had inherited a rather bad temper. She learned to control it, although she once threw a slipper at her chief minister. Even in later life she sometimes swore at her advisers.

Elizabeth was intelligent and artistic. Like her father, she loved music. She wanted to surround herself with people who were clever, witty and charming. The finest writers and musicians performed for Elizabeth and her court.

She ruled with great skill – like her father, but without his cruelty. At the start of her reign, she said, 'I care not for myself. My life is not dear to me, my care is for my people.'

She knew she faced problems. There was a real danger that the French or Spanish might attack. But Elizabeth was broke; she did not have the money to defend her people.

Above all, the country was torn by differences over religion. Most people accepted Elizabeth's solution. Whatever her own religious views, she kept very quiet about them.

There was the problem, too, of marriage. Parliament wanted her to marry. They felt the country would be safer if she did.

She was not short of men who wanted to marry her. At times, she seemed to be in love with one or other of them. One of her favourites was a Frenchman, the Duke of Alençon. He was less then half her age and his face was scarred by smallpox.

But the council did not want her to marry him. In the end, they give the Duke £10,000 to leave the country. Elizabeth later wrote that she would give a million pounds to see her Frog swimming once more in the Thames.

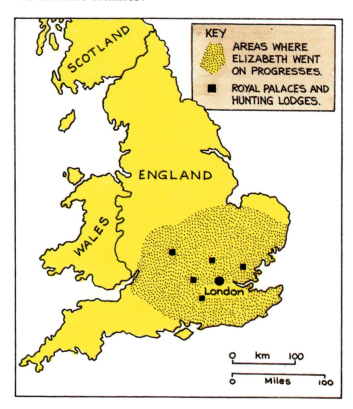

B Every summer, Elizabeth went on a *progress* but there were large areas which she never visited. Even her father went to the north only once, in 1541.

C Elizabeth I by Nicholas Hilliard, 1585. The animal on her sleeve is an ermine, a symbol of purity.

Elizabeth was England's only unmarried queen. Perhaps she knew that, if she married an English nobleman, she would offend others. If she had married a foreigner, she would not have been so free to follow her own policies.

And these policies *were* successful. When she died in 1603, England was one of the world's leading trading nations. It had also become a major power in Europe.

Above all, she handed over a country which was more peaceful and united than ever before. Many people thought she was wonderful. No wonder they looked back on her reign as a Golden Age.

Naturally, in such a golden age, people wanted to know what its queen looked like. People described her as 'handsome' but her face was pitted with smallpox scars; soon after she caught the disease, much of her hair fell out. In later life, she wore a red wig; her real hair was grey. After about 1584, she refused to look in a mirror.

Queen Elizabeth I was a favourite subject for painters. So we ought to have a good idea of what she looked like. But, as you can see from these pages, it is not as easy as that.

D M de Maisse, French Ambassador in England, described Elizabeth on two occasions in his diary (1597).

1 She was in a dress of silver cloth, white and crimson. She kept the front of her dress open, and often she would open the front of this robe with her hands as if she was too hot. She had a chain of rubies and pearls about her neck.

On her head she wore a garland of the same material and beneath it a great reddish wig. As for her face, it is very aged. It is long and thin, and her teeth are very yellow and unequal, compared with what they once were, so they say. On the left side there are less than on the right. Many of them are missing so that one cannot understand her when she speaks quickly.

Her figure is fair and tall and graceful in whatever she does.

All the time she spoke she would often rise from her chair, and appear to be very impatient with what I was saying. She told me that she was well pleased to stand up, and that she used to speak [like this] with the ambassadors who came to see her, and used sometimes to tire them, of which they would on occasion complain.

2 She had a petticoat of white, open in front, as was also her   chemise . When she raises her head she has a trick of putting both hands on her gown and opening it so that all her belly can be seen.

Accounts of the past may disagree. Sometimes, artists do not paint people or places exactly as they are. Paintings of Elizabeth I may not show her as she actually was but as she wanted people to think of her.

---

1 a) Write down all the words in the text which describe Elizabeth I as (i) a person and (ii) a ruler.
b) Now, write down the words which describe what she looked like.
c) Which of your three lists do you think is most important? Give reasons.

2 a) Study source A carefully. Why has the painter included the serpent?
b) The words on the left mean 'No rainbow without the sun'. Who do you think 'the sun' was?
c) What, then, do these words mean?

3 Look at sources A, C and D. Which do you think gives the most reliable idea of the queen's appearance? Explain how you decided.

4 a) Why do you think painters:
(i) did not show the queen without a wig?
(ii) did not show the queen looking older?
b) Why do you think the people who ordered these paintings did not want a lifelike portrait? Give at least two reasons.

A A contemporary painting of the court. The dancing lady may be the queen.

NOBLES AND GENTRY

B Philip Stubbes: *The Anatomie of Abuses* (1583).
No people in the world is so curious [of new fashions] as [the English]. So it is very difficult to know who is noble, who is a gentleman and who is not. For those who are [not] noble or gentry go daily in silks, velvets, satins and such like. This causes a great confusion.

Obviously, Stubbes did not like new fashions. But the source tells us something else. Elizabeth's people were very aware of their position in life. They believed that some people were of a higher class than others. And the greatest in the land were the nobles, such as lords and earls.

When there was war, the nobles led the army and navy. When England faced the Armada in 1588, Elizabeth had chosen Lord Howard to command the English navy. It was a job for a noble.

There were more gentry than nobles but they are less easy to pin down. Like the nobles, they did not work for a living: their money came from the land they owned. They either rented out their land or paid people to farm it for them. Meanwhile, the men spent their time hunting, eating and drinking. The ladies did embroidery or made lace.

Of course, people sometimes moved from one group to another. The younger sons of nobles became gentry. And there was always the chance that the queen would give a gentleman a title.

Elizabeth tended to pick her councillors from among the gentry. Others stayed at home and helped run their counties. They became justices of the peace (JPs). They helped keep law and order.

None of them got paid for this work. They thought it was a great honour to serve their queen. If she was pleased, she might reward them with more land or a new title.

If you wanted an important job, you had to attend the queen's court. This could be very expensive. Only those who were in the queen's service were given free lodgings at court. The rest had to pay.

Elizabeth's court did not stay in one place. When she went on a summer progress, her courtiers went with her. At night, she stayed at a noble's house so it cost her nothing. This meant she did not have to ask Parliament so often for money.

The queen expected to be looked after well. There might be musicians and actors to entertain her. Some lords even built an extension just for the occasion!

People had clear ideas about their position in life.

The hosts welcomed the queen with open arms. Behind her back, they grumbled. It could cost £1000 a day to put up the queen and all her courtiers. Apart from all the food, she loved playing cards – and hated losing!

Life at court was expensive even when the queen was not travelling. Elizabeth loved fine clothes; she left 1000 dresses when she died. She expected her courtiers to dress well, too.

The gentlemen, like the ladies, wore clothes of bright colours and materials such as silk and velvet. Precious jewels were sewn onto them. It is not surprising that many of the courtiers were deeply in debt.

The expense did not end there. The queen expected to be given presents. She especially liked unusual gifts. Someone once gave her a pair of black silk stockings. They were the first in England.

C These clothes belonged to Queen Elizabeth I. They are at Hatfield House, where she was living in 1558 when she heard she had become queen.

D Lady Margaret Hoby kept a diary from 1599 to 1605. These extracts give some idea of her life.

After private prayer I saw a man's leg dressed, took order for things in the house and [sewed] till dinner time. I exercised my body at bowls. Went about [making brandy].

Gave a poor woman [an ointment] for her arm.

After breakfast I was busy to dye wool.

I did busy myself about making of oil.

Bought a little spinning wheel and span of that.

After dinner I was busy weighing of wool till almost night.

Busy about wax lights. I did see lights made almost all the afternoon.

I went to take my bees and saw my honey ordered.

After I dined I talked and read to some good wives.

I walked with Mr Hoby about the town, to spy out the best places where cottages might be builded.

E Some of the New Year gifts given to Elizabeth I, 1588-9. (See note on page 2).

By Sir Christopher Hatton: a collar of gold.
By the Earl of Shrewsbury: in gold, £20.
By the Earl of Ormonde: part of a satin petticoat.
By the Countess of Lincoln: a long velvet cloak.
By the Countess of Bath: a fan of swan down.
By the Archbishop of Canterbury: in gold, £40.
By Sir Thomas Layton: a white petticoat.
By Sir Robert Sidney: a doublet of white satin.
By the Countess of Pembroke: in gold, £10.
By the Bishop of London: in gold, £20.
By the Earl of Sussex: in gold, £10.
By the Lord Hunsdon: part of the covering of a gown.

1 a) Who were (i) nobles and (ii) gentry?
   b) What was the difference between them?
   c) How did these people earn their living?
   d) Why were they willing to help run the country without being paid? (Give more than one answer.)

2 Look at sources A, C and E. What can you learn from them about:
   a) what the queen liked;
   b) how rich the nobles were;
   c) entertainment and
   d) fashion?

3 a) List the jobs which Lady Margaret did.
   b) Which of these tasks would a rich person not do today?
   c) Explain why you think they would not do them.
   d) What does the text tell you about ladies' lives?
   e) What can you learn from source D about Lady Margaret's life?
   f) Suggest at least two possible reasons for the difference.

MERCHANTS

One group of people was doing very well during the 16th century. They were the merchants who made their living by buying and selling goods.

The richest merchants of all were those in London. But smaller towns, too, had their merchants. Nicholas Chaffyn was one of them. He was a mercer with a shop in Salisbury early in the century. The shop was quite large; it had three rooms. Nicholas and his wife Agnes had five other rooms for their home.

There, they lived in greater comfort than their grandparents had ever done. The hall had green carpets, to match the seat covers. There were two chairs (instead of just stools) in the parlour.

When they went to bed, the Chaffyns used candles, instead of rush-lights. The Chaffyns were not rich enough to afford tapestries. But there were wall hangings in some rooms, including the bedroom. There were also feather beds with proper pillows and a mattress stuffed with wool.

Nicholas's shop sold all kinds of household goods, including soap and cloth. In 1513, he also had eight dozen glasses in stock. You could have bought the lot for 10p.

Traders were still organised in guilds, as they had been in the middle ages. But guilds were becoming less important. After 1563, local JPs, instead of the guilds, fixed wages each year. After that date, all apprentices had to serve their master or mistress for seven years.

However, apprentices were as rowdy as ever. Some carried wooden clubs slung round their necks. They used them to protect people from thieves. When no one was at risk, they went into a nearby street and used them to fight other apprentices.

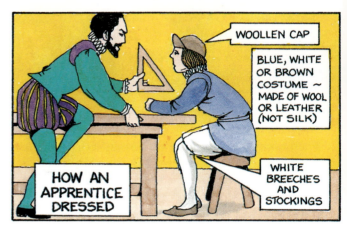

Each day, the bells of London rang out at 9 pm to tell the apprentices that their day's work was over. Apprentices lived with their master or mistress, usually over the shop. The apprentices often slept *in* the shop!

A few rich London merchants had tall houses of three or four storeys. They were beginning to have glass in their windows. Inside, it might have looked like this room, created in a London museum.

Even so, the gentry looked down on the merchants because they worked for a living. So the merchants were keen to buy land so they could join the ranks of the gentry. But the merchants, in their turn, looked down on others, as you shall see.

A A rich London merchant painted in 1532 by Holbein.

C The Salisbury Shoemakers' Guild met in this room after 1638.

D From a play called *The Four Apprentices*. An apprentice called Eustace has been asked by his father whether he likes the work. This is his reply.

Methinks I could endure it for seven years,
Did not my master keep me in too much.
I cannot go to breakfast in a morning
With my kind mates and fellow 'prentices,
But he cries 'Eustace!'; one bids Eustace come,
And my name Eustace is in every room.
I am no sooner got into the fencing school
To play a [match] with some friends I bring,
But 'Eustace! Eustace!' all the streets must ring.
He will not allow me one hour for sport,
I must not strike a football in the street,
But he will frown; nor view the dancing school,
But he will miss me straight; nor suffer me
So much as take up cudgels in the street,
But he will chide.

Historians study sources for evidence of change. They also look for signs of continuity. This means those things which have not changed over the years.

E William Powncett was a merchant who died in 1553. This is a list of his furnishings.

Hall (living-room):
First two tables, 2 [benches], 2 pairs of trestles 33p
Item 3 chairs, 12 joined stools 30p
Item 1 counter table and 1 round table 15p
Item the hangings of painted canvas £1.33
Item 5 great cushions with hearts 25p
Item 3 carpets 30p
Item a Bible in English 12.5p
Item a curtain for the window 2.5p
Item 3 war bills (weapons) 90p

Parlour:
First, hangings and the curtains of the windows in red and green, say 50p
Item a joined table, [another] table and a short square table 66.5p
Item 2 chairs of walnut-tree, one covered with green cloth and the seat of the other of green velvet 33p
Item 6 joined stools, 2 low stools covered with green cloth and 7 foot-stools 23p
Item a screen of [twigs] 2.5p
Item 6 cushions with roses 30p
Item 6 cushions of crewel (fine wool), 3 small crewel cushions and 3 long and silk £1.82
Item 5 carpets £1.50
Item a joined chair 3p
Item 2 cobirons (to hold up the spit), 1 pair of tongs, 1 fire shovel, 6 pots and a plate of iron in the chimney 66p

1. From the text on page 16, write down one example of change and one of continuity.
2. a) Read about Nicholas Chaffyn on page 16. Write down three ways in which his house was more comfortable than a house in the middle ages.
   b) In what way was his home less comfortable than yours?
   c) How was his hall more comfortable than the room in source B?
3. a) How would you expect a modern merchant's clothes to differ from those in source A?
   b) Look very carefully. What else would be different nowadays?
4. a) Look at source C. What do you think has changed since 1638? Explain how you decided.
   b) Do you think this is still used for guild meetings? Give reasons.
5. a) Read source E. Write down five objects you have in your living room which he did not own. Suggest reasons why he did not own them.
   b) Which objects are both in his list and in your home?
6. Read source D. Do you think apprentices had changed much since the middle ages? Give reasons.

DOWN ON THE FARM

The gentry looked down on the merchants. And the merchants, in turn, looked down on the yeomen, who were farmers. They either owned a small farm of their own or rented land from someone else.

Like the gentry, the yeomen were important figures in their villages. However, there was one major difference between a yeoman and a gentleman. A gentleman was expected to live and dress like a gentleman – and this cost money. He had a fine home to keep up and many servants to run it.

But the yeoman was less worried about what people thought of him. He did not need to wear a gentleman's fine clothes to impress other gentlemen. A typical yeoman's clothes were woven at home by his wife. They were often blue or brown, like an apprentice's costume.

Instead, the yeoman could invest his money in his farm. Elizabeth's reign was a good time for the yeomen: food prices were rising.

The position of a yeoman might vary. But there was no doubt about who ranked the lowest in society. These were the labourers. They were no better off than peasants in the middle ages.

Most of these labourers lived in the country. They included village craftsmen, such as the smith and the carpenter. (The better-off craftworkers in towns ranked alongside the merchants.)

Today, labourers get a living from earning wages. Tudor labourers usually had some land as well. They would grow their own vegetables, keep chickens and perhaps have a few pigs.

Probably more than half the population lived in real poverty. When times were really hard, they made their bread out of acorns. Bad luck or old age could bring death from starvation.

A This house at Bignor in Sussex was once owned by a yeoman.

A hard-working yeoman could buy land from gentry who needed the money. In time, his family might even join the ranks of the gentry. On the other hand, a gentleman who wasted his money might end up renting land as a yeoman.

B This French picture shows a carpenter at work in about 1490.

C A painting of Morris dancers beside the River Thames (early 17th century).

Historians first have to find their sources. The second job is to understand them. Old-fashioned words and spellings can sometimes make this difficult.

D This 17th-century **inventory** listed the goods of Bartholomew Burch.

In the hall: one table, one cupboard, one kneading trough[1], ten chairs, a pair of pot hangers, a pair of tongs, a gridiron, a salt box

In the milk house: five tongs, six bowls, three plates, a pair of scales

In the hall chamber: one bed and bedstead, three bolsters, four blankets, one coverlet, [one moveable bed], one linen and one woollen trendell[2], four chests

In the drink house: three tubs, two barrels and other old lumber and a churn

One hay cutter, one hand saw and a mattock[3]

Boards and shelves and old lumber

Outside: wood, hay and large barrels

Three cows, one hog and a birding piece[4]

Things unseen and forgotten

[1] a trough for turning flour into dough for bread [2] wheel for spinning [3] pickaxe with one flat end [4] for catching birds

E The gap between rich and poor showed up clearly in their meals. William Harrison outlined them in *Description of England* (1577).

The nobles, gentry and students do [usually] go to dinner at eleven and to supper at five, or between five and six in the afternoon. The merchants dine and sup seldom before twelve noon and six at night, especially in London. The farmers dine also at high noon and sup at seven or eight. As for the poorest, they generally dine or sup when they [can], so to talk of their order of [meals] is useless.

Please work in pairs.

1. a) What were the differences between a gentleman and a yeoman?
   b) How did each earn his living? (Answer carefully.)

2. a) Look at source C. Write the numbers 1-8 on separate lines.
   b) Decide whether each person lived in the town or country. Beside each number, write either 'town person' or 'country person'.
   c) Explain how you decided.

3. a) Read source D. How could you tell that this man worked in the countryside?
   b) Is he better off or worse off than William Powncett (source E on page 17)? Explain how you decided.
   c) Do you think he was a yeoman or a labourer? Give reasons.
   d) Do you think the carpenter in source B would have ranked alongside a merchant or below him? Explain how you decided.

PAUPERS AND VAGABONDS

A This dole cupboard can still be seen at Haddon Hall in Derbyshire. Bread was put here to give to the poor.

Probably half the population lived in real poverty in the 16th century. But there was one group of people who were even worse off than the poorest labourers. These were the paupers.

A pauper is a person without a job who relies on charity. Many wandered the roads of the land. Some were looking for work; some earned a living from crime; most of them begged. People called them vagabonds.

One Elizabethan writer said he had heard that there were 10,000 of them. Of course, that could have just been a guess. There was no way anyone could have counted them. But the figure shows that people thought the problem was serious.

The rich had never seen anything like it and they were frightened. In the middle ages, being out of work was rare. Most people worked on a manor. The lord of the manor was expected to look after his peasants.

Tudor people had a very clear idea of people's ranks – and these vagabonds just didn't fit into the system. Tramps were seen as enemies; you could be fined for sheltering a stranger.

B Three kinds of beggar, copied from a drawing of Henry VIII's reign.

The vagabonds were certainly a mixed bunch. Some were genuine gypsies; they had first arrived in England in about 1500. Others were ex-soldiers or farm labourers who had fallen on hard times. Others were just criminals.

A whole gang of them might descend on a village and scare the living daylights out of the villagers. In the end, the villagers might pay money or give them food just to get rid of them. In 1581, riding out towards Islington, even the queen found herself surrounded by such a gang.

The government had no more idea of how to solve the problem than the villagers did. Many people thought that being unemployed was a sin. So they did not look for ways of solving the unemployment problem. Instead, they looked for ways of punishing the vagabonds.

This was yet another problem. There was no proper police force. There were not many gaols, either. So punishments were usually short, sharp and in public.

Tudor governments passed one Act of Parliament after another to deal with the problem. In 1601, they produced the Poor Law. This Act laid down how paupers were to be dealt with. It did not change much for over 200 years.

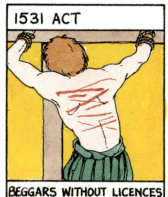

1531 ACT — BEGGARS WITHOUT LICENCES WERE WHIPPED

1547 ACT — VAGABONDS BRANDED AND MADE SLAVES

1562 ACT — PEOPLE MADE TO GIVE HELP

1572 ACT — EVERYONE HAD TO PAY A POOR RATE

C The government did not help the unemployed and sick, as it does today. Instead, it passed these Acts to try and solve the problem.

1. PAUPER CHILDREN — TO BE APPRENTICED
2. SICK PAUPERS — LOOKED AFTER AT HOME OR IN SPECIAL HOUSES
3. ABLE-BODIED POOR — GIVEN WORK
4. IDLE POOR — SENT TO HOUSES OF CORRECTION (WORKHOUSES)

D The poor in St Nicholas's parish, Ipswich, 1597. 'Relief' means the amount of money they were being given. 'Wants' means what these people need.

Names and conditions	Ages	Works	Wage	Children	Ages	Works	Relief	Wants
An Thaxter	54	Knits Stockings	2		12 9	Knit Stockings	3p	3p Clothing
Robert Edwards Feeble-minded	40	Shears Woollen Cloth	2				3p	5p
His wife, able but presently sick	30							
John Tassell, able	40	Weaver	4		8 6 4 2			Worke 1½p
His wife, able	50							
Robinson, able		A knacker	4					5p Clothing, Firing
His wife, great with child								
Symon Blith, blind	65		2		8		4p	5p
His wife	60				8		3p	Firing
An Jacksonne, widow	60	Gathers rushes					2½p	2½p
Widow Goffe	40	A sewer	4		14 13 5 2	Sews	1½p	5p
John Wilson		Labourer	10p	3	7 5 2	Spins		2½p Wheels and Cards
His wife		Spins wool						
Reynald Clark	65	Taylor	2		14 12		3p	3p Firing
His wife	40							
An Martin		Spins flax					3p	3p

Historians must ask various questions about their sources. The questions include:
- when was the source made?
- why was it made?
- what can we learn from this source?
- what can we *not* learn from it?

The answers will help a historian to decide how useful the source is.

E The 1601 Poor Law said there were four different kinds of paupers. Each was to be treated differently.

F In the 17th century, a new solution was found. This record explains what was done in Liverpool (1648).

[Various] young children and beggars are found wandering and begging against the law. Therefore, the Mayor [and council] shall go through the town and take their names and examine them. Such as are able to work [shall] be shipped for Barbados. If they belong to this town, [they shall be made] apprentices.

1 a) Draw a timeline for the years 1510–1610. Use one centimetre for each decade.
b) Mark on your timeline each Act of Parliament mentioned on these pages.
2 This question is about source D.
a) When was source D written?
b) Why do you think source D was written?
c) What can you learn from this source about why some people were poor?
d) What can you learn from this source about how the poor were dealt with?
e) After 1601, which of Widow Goffe's children do you think would have been apprenticed? Explain your answer carefully.
f) What trade were most of these people involved in?
g) Why would a historian want to see figures from other towns before deciding how bad the problem was?
h) How useful is this source for someone studying poverty in the 16th century? Give reasons for your answer.

WHY WERE THERE SO MANY POOR?

Another question which historians ask is: Why did events happen in the past? What *caused* them? Why were there more people out of work in Queen Elizabeth's reign? Some of the causes were more important than others.

Writers in the 16th century were quite clear why so many people were not working. They wrote masses of leaflets about it. Priests gave their views in Sunday sermons and Parliament often discussed it. However, they did not agree.

Ever since, historians have been trying to work it out – and they have not always agreed, either. These are some of the causes which have been suggested.

1 Enclosures

A Philip Stubbes wrote in 1583:
These enclosures be the causes why rich men eat up poor men as beasts do eat grass.

Many landowners had fenced in the great open fields in the villages. It had started happening in the middle ages. It speeded up in the 16th century. Often, the common land was enclosed, too. That meant that the peasants had nowhere to graze their sheep and cattle. In future, they would have to work for wages.

B One use of the land around the village is shown in this medieval picture.

2 Sheep farming

C John Aubrey, writing in the 17th century:
A shepherd and his dog can manage the land that [once] employed several scores of labourers.

Some landowners gave up growing crops and kept sheep instead. English and Welsh wool was in great demand abroad. So there was always money to be made from keeping sheep. But there were fewer jobs on a sheep farm.

D This picture appeared in the *Shepheard's Calendar* (1597).

3 There were more people

E This graph shows an estimate of how the population of England was growing. No accurate counts were made at the time.

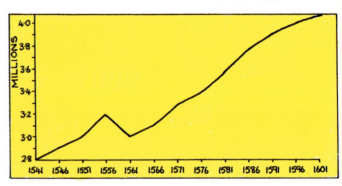

4 There was inflation

Prices went up – and they kept going up. We call this inflation. Prices at least trebled during the 16th century. The poorest people suffered most. They were almost certainly worse off than their grandparents had been.

William Harrison gave examples of how prices rose during the century:

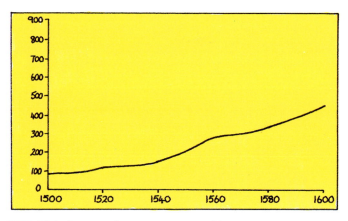

F This is a modern estimate of how prices rose during the 16th century.

5 Gambling

G Some people said gambling was a cause of poverty. This picture comes from *Shyppe of Fools* (1517).

6 The End of Wars

The country was at war for much of the 15th century. The fighting ended in 1485. In 1487, Henry VII forced the barons to get rid of their private armies. All of a sudden, many soldiers found themselves out of work.

H In 1594, William Lambarde wrote:
> Is it [surprising] after they return from the wars, that they either lead their lives in begging, or end them in hanging?

7 The monasteries were closed

In 1536-40, Henry VIII closed down the monasteries. In the past, monks and nuns had helped the poor and sick. Now, they could not. Not only that – many of their servants were now without jobs.

I Arable farming employed more people than sheep farming, especially at busy times such as harvest (16th century).

Working in groups, think about the question 'Why were there so many poor in 16th century England?'

1. a) List each possible cause on a separate line.
   b) For each one, give a mark out of ten to show how important you think it was. (The most important gets the highest mark.)
   c) Look at your highest and lowest marks. Explain how you decided about these.

2. a) Look at graphs E and F. Which came first – rising prices or a rise in the population? Explain how you decided.
   b) Look at sources B, D and I. Which do you think was more likely to lose people their jobs – enclosure or sheep farming? Explain how you decided.
   c) Look carefully at source F. Does it prove that closing the monasteries caused prices to rise or not? Explain how you decided.
   d) Read the caption to source E. Why would the Tudors have found it hard to understand why unemployment was rising?

THE PLAYERS (ACTORS)

In the middle ages, mystery plays were the only kind of drama many people ever saw. In these plays, local people paraded through the streets of their town and acted out stories from the Bible.

But the religious changes of the 16th century meant that many people no longer approved of these plays. Queen Mary had liked them but Queen Elizabeth frowned on them.

As a result, playwrights wrote different kinds of plays, including comedies. Groups of players travelled around the country, performing them. They might turn up once or twice a year in a village to act their plays in the courtyard of an inn or on the village green.

Elizabeth's people loved music and drama and the queen enjoyed plays as much as anyone. She used to command players to come to her palace and act for her. Londoners were also lucky. From about 1575 onwards, playhouses were built near London. One of these was the Globe Theatre and one of its actors was a young man called William Shakespeare.

B The Globe Theatre, opened in 1599.

Today, most people agree that Shakespeare is the greatest playwright of all time. Yet many young people find reading a Shakespeare play difficult. They are not used to the words or phrases he used. However, the Elizabethans, too, did not understand everything he wrote.

The reason is that the Elizabethans took a delight in words. Perhaps that seems a strange thing to say. But the Elizabethans enjoyed making up new words and finding new uses for old ones.

Shakespeare was no exception. Have you ever been 'tongue-tied' or 'laughed yourself into stitches'? Has a teacher ever told you it's 'high time' you vanished into 'thin air'? Have your 'own flesh and blood' ever 'sent you packing'? All these phrases first appeared in a Shakespeare play.

There is another reason why a Shakespeare play is hard to understand. English people in his time did not all speak the same English. Shakespeare was born in Stratford-upon-Avon so he would have spoken Midlands English. He moved to London and became an actor. In London, they spoke the English which Caxton used in his books. Shakespeare's plays use both kinds of English.

His plays tell us a great deal about how people lived and thought in Elizabethan times. They show us how much the people loved their country. They felt proud of England and excited to be English.

A William Shakespeare. Of all the portraits of him, this is probably the most accurate. His plays use 30,000 different words, twice the number used by an educated person today.

C T Platter described a visit to a playhouse in *Travels in England* (1599).

Daily at two in the afternoon, London has two, sometimes three, plays running. Those which play best obtain most spectators.

They play on a raised platform, so that everyone has a good view. There are different galleries where the seating is more comfortable and therefore more expensive. Whoever cares to stand below only pays one English penny. But if he wishes to sit, he enters by another door, and pays another penny. If he desires to sit in the most comfortable seats, which are cushioned, where he not only sees everything well, but can also be seen, he pays yet another.

During the performance food and drink are carried round the audience. The actors are expensively dressed; it is the English custom for Lords or Knights to leave almost the best of their clothes to their servants. It is [not suitable for them] to wear [these], so they offer them for sale to the actors.

D This drawing of the Swan Theatre, in about 1596, is the only contemporary picture of the inside of an Elizabethan theatre. It is based on an eye-witness drawing.

Religious changes affected plays, just as they affected everyday life. Mystery plays went out of fashion. The Catholics approved of them; many Protestants did not.

1. Answer these questions in sentences:
   a) Why did mystery plays go out of fashion?
   b) Where were the early plays performed?
   c) Why are Shakespeare's plays not easy to understand?
   d) What can we learn about Elizabethan people from the plays?
2. a) Is source D a primary or secondary source? Explain how you know.
   b) How can you tell this is the Swan Theatre?
   c) Write down all the ways it is different to a modern theatre.
   d) How is it the same?
3. What problems did it create for the actors:
   a) Having little scenery?
   b) Having no curtain?
   c) Having people eating and drinking during a performance?
   d) Having no electric light?

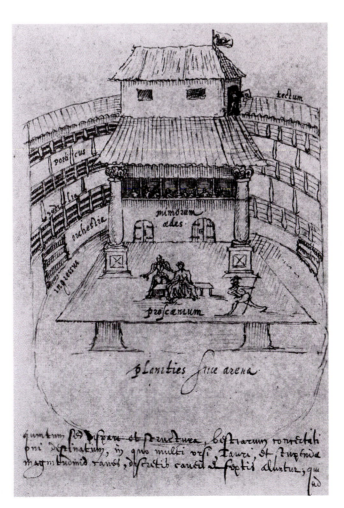

Thatched roof. (The Globe burned down in 1613.)

A seat in the gallery (known as the gods) cost 1p.

There was no stage curtain.

There were no female actors in the 16th century.

Money was collected and put into locked boxes. This is why we still talk of a *box office*.

The flag meant a play was being acted.

Early theatres were built like the inn courtyards where players were used to acting.

There was little scenery.

Standing room in the pit cost ½p.

People sold pies, soup and ale. The audience ate and drank during the play.

5 MORE RELIGIOUS PROBLEMS

The Scottish king, James V, had not changed his religion, as Henry VIII had done. He stayed Roman Catholic and was loyal to the Pope. So was his daughter, Mary, when she became Queen of the Scots.

Mary was Elizabeth's cousin and heir. If Elizabeth had no children, Mary would become the next Queen of England. That might have been no problem if Mary had stayed in Scotland. But in 1567, her husband, Lord Darnley, was killed in an explosion just outside Edinburgh.

Many people thought Earl Bothwell had planned Darnley's death. Yet, three months later, Mary married him. Within a month, there was a rebellion. Bothwell fled abroad but Mary was taken prisoner. She was forced to give up the throne to her infant son, James VI. They are shown together in this later painting.

A year later, she cut off her red hair so that no one would recognise her and she sailed from Scotland to England. Elizabeth made her a prisoner – and a prisoner she stayed for the next 19 years.

Throughout that time, Elizabeth still grappled with the problem of religion. Although most English people accepted the Church of England, even some Protestants wished to change it.

These were the Puritans. They got this name because they wished to purify the Church of England. In other words, they wanted to rid it of those things they thought were wrong.

As the years passed, they found more and more they did not like. They did not approve of bishops running the Church. Nor did they like the churches themselves. They wanted to get rid of altars, candles and other decorations. They did not think much of the services, either. They wanted more preaching and different prayers.

None of this would have mattered if they had just wanted these things for themselves. But the Puritans wanted everyone to be Puritan. Quite a few MPs were Puritan, so Puritan views could not be ignored.

However, the Puritans were not a danger to Elizabeth. The Catholics were. As far as they were concerned, Elizabeth was a heretic. It was the duty of all good English Catholics to make their homeland Catholic once again.

Elizabeth had been tolerant towards Catholics when she became queen. But, in the 1570s, a number of English Catholics returned to England. Their job was to persuade people to become Catholic.

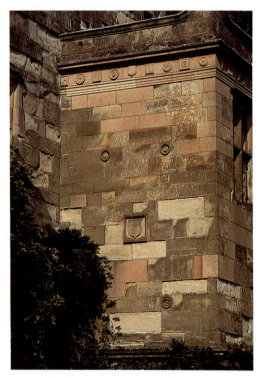

B This secret sign is called a quincunx. It was placed by the doorway in Catholic homes so a priest would know he could safely knock. It is a symbol of the five wounds of Christ. This one can still be seen at Bentham Hall, Shropshire

This scene is in an imaginary Elizabethan house, owned by Catholics. See question 2.

Parliament decided to act. In 1581, it said that anyone not going to church would be fined £20 a month. Anyone not paying the fine would go to prison. There were about 100 Catholic priests in England at the time. Rich Catholic families did what they could to protect them; some built secret hiding places in their homes. A few of these can still be seen today.

Some priests were caught; a few were charged with treason and executed. Despite this, Catholic plots were a lasting threat. And, like it or not, Mary was at the centre of some of them. After all, she was the obvious choice as Catholic monarch.

In 1586, Sir Francis Walsingham, the queen's minister, finally trapped Mary. She was put on trial and found guilty of plotting to kill Elizabeth. In February 1587, Elizabeth at last signed the death warrant. The sentence was carried out quickly before Elizabeth changed her mind.

1. Write one sentence about each of these words: heir; heretic; Puritan; quincunx.

2. a) Look at the picture above. Imagine that two priests are hiding here, along with the valuables used in their services. (They are shown above, on the right.) Where are they?
   b) Are they good hiding-places or not? Give reasons.

3. a) Look at this list of ways of hiding a Catholic priest. Write each one down and give it a mark out of ten.
   (i) a false panel in a wall; (ii) up the chimney; (iii) a secret passage; (iv) under the stairs; (v) in a barrel; (vi) in the loft; (vii) in the garden; (viii) in the kitchen; (ix) disguised as a servant.
   b) Give reasons for your top choice.

6 THE ARMADA: A GREAT VICTORY?

1500 1525 1550 1575 1600 1625 1650 1675 1700 1725 1750

A This painting shows the English and Spanish fleets at war. It was painted in about 1590.

Perhaps the most famous event of Elizabeth's reign came in 1588 when the Spanish fleet set sail for England. The story has been told countless times in school textbooks. Often, it has gone something like this. (The written sources are all from textbooks and are listed under the questions.)

The King of Spain was Philip II, who had once been Queen Mary I's husband. Long after her death, he wanted England to become Catholic again. The solution seemed to be to invade England.

B As a result he began to make plans for a great fleet, or 'Armada', which would sweep up the English Channel, clear it of Elizabeth's ships and then transport his army from the Netherlands to England. The army, commanded by the Duke of Parma, was already in the Netherlands.

By April 1587, Philip's Armada was nearly ready. Then, the English captain Drake sailed into Cadiz harbour and destroyed many of the boats. As a result, the Armada did not sail for another year.

C This was a disastrous delay, because his admiral died in the winter. He gave the command instead to the Duke of Medina Sidonia. [He] had had no experience of the sea, and proved quite unsuitable.

At its second attempt, the Armada headed for England in July 1588. It was a huge fleet of at least 130 ships. It appeared in the Channel on 19 July. The ships were drawn up in a crescent shape which was difficult to attack.

D It took over a week for the great navy to sail up the Channel, and all the time there was a running fight with the English fleet under Lord Howard and Drake.

E Each fleet had roughly the same number of galleons But while the Spanish ships were tall and heavy, English galleons were low and slim. They were faster too and could turn more easily.

On 27 July, the Armada anchored near Calais, where they intended to pick up the troops who would invade England. This gave the English the chance they needed.

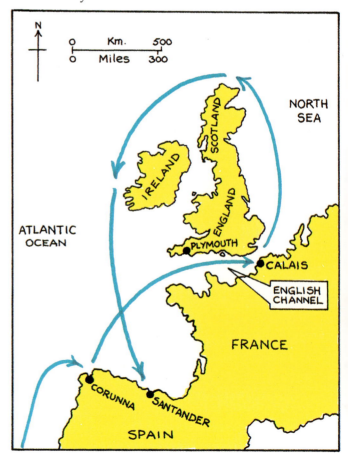

F The route taken by the Armada.

It was a great victory for the English. Philip II had been sure that God was on *his* side. Queen Elizabeth was now sure that God had been on *her* side. She may have written a poem which includes these words: 'He made the winds and waters rise to scatter all mine enemies.'

K This medal was made for Prince Maurice, the Dutch commander-in-chief. The words say: 'God blew and they were scattered'. Throughout Europe, people believed that God had helped the English to win.

> Religion was involved in almost every aspect of life in the 16th century. This event is no exception.

G Queen Elizabeth I is shown in this panel from St Faith's Church, Gaywood. It says: 'Blessed be the great God of my Salvation '. It was painted after the Armada returned to Spain.

H Lord Howard . . . sent eight fire-ships into the Spanish fleet at night, forcing the Spanish ships to cut their anchor cables and drift out into the open sea. The following morning . . . Howard ordered his own ships to attack. The small, fast English warships were more than a match for the lumbering Spanish galleons crowded with troops.

The Duke of Medina Sidonia had no choice but to head for home. So he headed north, planning to sail round Scotland. It would be a long journey back but he knew there was no chance of fighting his way back down the Channel.

Safe from the English, the ships sailed round Scotland. But they were not safe from the weather. Great storms drove the Armada onto the rocky Scottish shore; yet more were destroyed off the Irish coast.

J Three months after they had set out with 130 proud ships, the fleet limped home with a little over 60 of their vessels afloat and more than half of the crews dead. The Armada had been defeated so completely that Spain never dared to threaten England again.

1 What do the text and sources tell you about:
a) the Armada's commander?
b) the Spanish ships?
c) why the Armada sailed?
d) what happened in the Channel?
e) what the results were?

2 a) What religion was Elizabeth I?
b) What religion was Philip II?
c) Think carefully. Why did each monarch want people to think God was on their side?
d) Why couldn't God be on both their sides?

3 a) Why did the English win, according to:
(i) Elizabeth I, (ii) source G and (iii) source K?
b) Do you think Philip II would have given the same reason? Again, explain your answer.
c) If the sources all give the same reason, does that mean it must be right? Explain carefully.
d) Look back at your answers to question 1. How could a historian find out if this information is correct?

Sources
A and H *The Tudors* by S L Case (1975); C and D *England and Europe* by M R Dacombe and V M S Heigham (1933); E *Life in Elizabethan Times* by David Whitehall (1990); J *History Alive* by Peter Moss (1969).

...OR NOT?

A A Spanish map, showing the British Isles, made in about 1555-60.

What you have just read is a fairly typical version of what happened to the Armada. You will probably find history books in your library which say much the same thing.

But how much of it is true?

> Historians must check *all* the sources. Sometimes, accounts of past events may be different from what really happened. Historians must always be on the lookout for propaganda.

B Hans Buttber, a German merchant, saw the fleets in the Channel. He wrote this:
> The fleets [fought on and off] and fired heavily at each other, but they could not board. The English, with their little ships, sailed so well and moved about so skilfully while they kept firing that the galleasses could not get at them.

Buttber was an eye-witness. He says quite clearly that the ships were firing at each other. Yet Spanish documents prove that the Spanish hardly ever fired their cannon. Buttber also writes about the 'little ships' of the English. Yet, in the 20th century, historians have studied the ships in the two fleets. One of them came up with some interesting statistics about the biggest ones:

C

Ship	Guns	Men	Tons
Triumph (English)	67	500	1100
San Juan (Spanish)	50	522	1050
Bear (English)	80	500	1000
San Martin (Spanish)	48	469	1000
Elizabeth Jonas (English)	76	500	900
San Luis (Spanish)	38	439	830
San Felipe (Spanish)	40	439	800
Victory (English)	64	400	800
Ark (English)	–	425	800

The Spanish commander, the Duke of Medina Sidonia, was not a complete novice at sea, either. He was also a good organiser. Very little had been done during the winter of 1587-8 to get the Armada ready. Yet, three months after the Duke was given the job, the Armada put to sea. It had more ships, more men and more guns than the fleet of 1587.

However, he was certainly against the whole idea of the Armada. He thought the plan was hopeless. So, too, did the Duke of Parma, who was to lead the invasion of England. As one commander put it, they were hoping for a miracle. According to Philip II, of course, God was on their side.

> Please work in pairs.
> 1. a) Look at source C. Who had the biggest ships? Answer carefully.
>   b) Be careful! Which of these people would have known these figures at the time: the fleets' commanders; Elizabeth I; Philip II; the English people; the Spanish people? Give reasons.
>   c) Why might the English at the time want people to think that the Spanish ships were more powerful?
> 2. Compare what it says about the Duke of Medina Sidonia on this page with page 28. What is the difference?
> 3. a) Now, write down how the two pages disagree about the ships.
>   b) Which do you think is correct? Give reasons.

The truth is that the Armada was short of men and equipment. It did not have enough soldiers to attack England directly; nor did it have enough ships to pick up the Duke of Parma's troops. It was short of powder; the wine was going off; the fish went rotten almost as soon as the ships left port.

So why did it go at all?

The picture on the next page gives some clues.

D This painting shows the defeat of the Spanish Armada. It was painted in about 1610. The English person (bottom right) holds the flag of St George.

E This picture was painted in 1579. It is full of symbols. The cow stands for the Netherlands. Philip II is on its back (a burden for the country); the Spanish Commander in the Netherlands is milking it (to get out of it whatever Spain can); Elizabeth I is feeding it (helping the country with troops and money). The French are interfering at the back and you can see the results.

King Philip II wanted to stop Elizabeth I interfering in the Netherlands; he also wanted to get English pirates away from the West Indies where they had been attacking Spanish ships.

A huge fleet which threatened England seemed to be the answer. Philip II had twice tried, and failed, to put an Armada to sea. This one simply had to sail – in order to frighten England.

It was certainly not sent to fight the English fleet. The Duke of Medina Sidonia's orders were quite clear: he had to avoid a battle if he possibly could. In fact, the Spanish doubted whether it would come to a battle. They thought the sheer size of the fleet would frighten the English.

The Armada's defeat was not a great English naval victory. Four battles were fought in the English Channel yet only one Spanish ship was actually sunk by gunfire. The Duke kept his fleet together until the fire-ships attacked. And the Armada *did* reach Calais, even though there was no invasion.

Of course, Spanish losses were high. About 60 per cent of the Spanish died. But so did more than half the English, after it was all over. Poor food, disease and neglect killed them.

Naturally, the English claimed a great victory. After all, there had been no invasion. But the fighting did not end. And the cost of wars against Spain was huge – about 1.5 million pounds.

Nor was the risk of attack over. The Spanish may have lost half their fleet but, by 1590, it was up to 100 ships again. Twice more, an Armada sailed for England; on each occasion, storms drove the ships back home. Peace was not agreed until 1604. By then, England had a new monarch.

---

4 a) What was the Armada's purpose, according to page 28?
b) What was the Armada's purpose, according to this page?
c) Which answer would the English government want people to believe – and why?
d) Which answer would the Spanish government want people to believe – and why?
e) How do pages 29 and 31 disagree about the results of the Armada?

5 a) Look at source D. How is the Armada shown?
b) Read the caption. Why is the Armada shown like this?
c) What message was the painter giving?

6 Compare source A with a modern map. How can this source help to explain what happened to the Armada? Give reasons.

7 KING JAMES AND THE GUNPOWDER PLOT

1525 1550 1575 1600 1625 1650 1675 1700 1725 1750

A 'Penny for the guy!' The original guys were models of the Pope. James I asked people to light bonfires on November 5th.

In March 1603, the church bells of London fell silent as the queen lay dying. The last of Henry VIII's children eventually passed away on 24 March. She died, as one writer put it, 'easily like a ripe apple from a tree'.

Queen Elizabeth had had no children. So the new monarch was her cousin, James VI of Scotland. Unlike the dead queen, he cared little for cheering crowds or making himself popular.

In any case, James was soon to find out that he could not please everybody. One reason, yet again, was religion. During Elizabeth's reign, most people had grown used to the new Church of England and its services. However, Roman Catholics and Puritans had not.

The Catholics hoped that James would allow them to worship in their own way. At first, he *did* stop fining those who didn't attend Church of England services. Then, he changed his mind and the fines returned.

Some Catholics thought that only a Catholic monarch would let them worship freely. James I was not Catholic. So, in 1604, a group of Catholic nobles decided to do something about it.

B This was what happened, according to Robert Cecil, the king's chief minister:

The plan was the idea of Robert Catesby, a Catholic. Along with other Catholic gentlemen[1], they would blow up the Houses of Parliament when King James I went there to make a speech[2].

In spring 1605, Thomas Percy rented a cellar[3] nearby. It led under the House of Lords. Barrels of gunpowder[4] were brought in and covered with wood and coal. The group had brought in Guy Fawkes, a Yorkshire gentleman and ex-soldier, to set the powder off. Meanwhile, the rest went to their country homes and waited. James was due to open Parliament on 5 November.

At 7 o'clock on 26 October, Lord Monteagle[5] was about to have dinner when one of his servants brought him a letter[6]. It had been given to him by a stranger in the street. The letter was written by Francis Tresham[7], one of the plotters and Lord Monteagle's cousin.

The letter warned him not to attend Parliament. 'They shall receive,' it said, 'a terrible blow'. Monteagle did not really know what to make of it. Even so, he took it at once to Robert Cecil, the King's chief minister[8]. Cecil took the letter to the King.

On 4 November, the cellar was searched. They found a heap of coal and wood. There was also a man who said he was called John Johnson. That evening, the cellar was searched again. This time, they found the gunpowder, too. John Johnson was arrested[9]. In the Tower of London, he was tortured and admitted that he was Guy Fawkes. He confessed about the plot on 8 November[10].

The other plotters were tracked down to the Midlands. A number, including Catesby and Percy[11], were shot dead[12]. One called Rokewood[13], was taken prisoner.

The survivors, including Fawkes, were found guilty of high treason. In January 1606, they were dragged to the place of execution. There, they were hanged, drawn and quartered. Their hearts were cut out and their insides burned in public.

You have just read one version of what happened. But historians must always ask if there is any other possible interpretation of an event. Source D gives some facts about the Gunpowder Plot which might suggest a different story.

Historians also study people's motives. The plotters were willing to kill the king, which was a political act. Their motives were religious – they wanted a Catholic monarch.

You should ask: what were Cecil's motives?

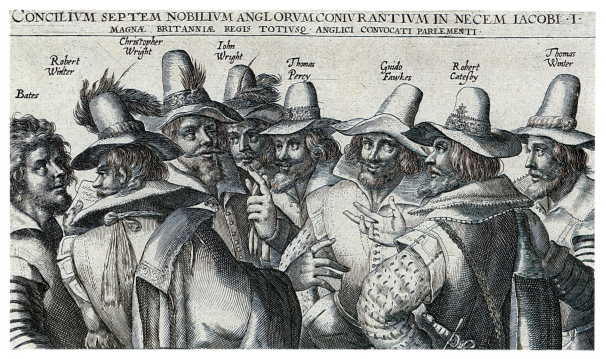

C The plotters are shown in this Dutch picture, made soon afterwards. It is unlikely that the artist actually saw them.

D Source B gives the government's version of the events. However, modern historians can add other details. Some of these were not known at the time. These notes give some extra details. (The numbers refer to those in source B.)

1 Cecil's spies were constantly watching leading Catholics.
2 This was originally planned for 7 February, then put off until 3 October; it was delayed again until 5 November.
3 This was owned by a government official who died suddenly on 5 November.
4 All gunpowder was kept in the Tower of London. You needed a licence to buy it. Cecil forbade any investigation into the Tower stores beyond early 1604.
5 Monteagle's name was removed from all accounts given by the plotters. Monteagle himself was given a pension, probably worth £40,000 a year in modern money.
6 Some modern handwriting experts think this letter was forged.
7 Francis Tresham was not arrested until later. He died in the Tower of London on 23 December. No one knows how.
8 Parliament was not due to meet for another ten days.
9 Cecil gave three different accounts of his arrest. This was just one of them.
10 His confession differs from the government's version.
11 The killer of Percy was given a pension of 10p a day for life.
12 They were surrounded by hundreds of armed men. The plotters were unarmed.
13 Rokewood's servant had *already* been arrested, early on 5 November.

---

1 a) Work in pairs. Read the notes above. Write down any details you found strange. Explain why you thought this.
b) Why would it have been strange if Cecil had *not* known about the plot?

2 a) What evidence is there that Cecil knew about the plot *before the Monteagle letter*?
b) What evidence is there that Cecil knew who was involved *before 5 November*?
c) Why might Cecil have wanted the main plotters shot dead?
d) Why do you think Tresham was not put on trial with the others?
f) Write down any weaknesses in Cecil's version in source B.
g) Write down your own version of what you think happened.

3 a) What were the plotters' motives?
b) If Cecil knew there was a plot, what were his motives in letting it continue?
c) What were people's motives for burning a figure of the Pope?
d) What were James's motives for wanting them to do this?

4 Depending on the time available, some of you could do a class presentation of your answers to question 1.

8 KING AND PARLIAMENT DISAGREE

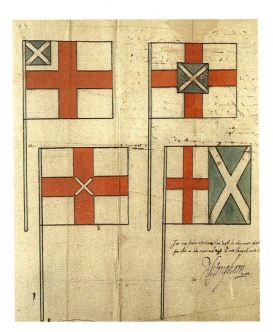

A King James was the first monarch to call himself King of Great Britain. There was the problem of how to unite the English and Scottish flags. These were some suggestions.

Religion was not James's only problem. There was also Parliament to deal with. Elizabeth I had believed that Parliament should only talk about those things which she wanted it to talk about. The members of Parliament thought differently. They wanted to discuss anything they felt like.

But Elizabeth I had been tactful and a popular queen. James I was tactless and not popular in England. Elizabeth had wanted to rule but she had not spent time talking about it. James also wanted to rule but he *did* believe in talking about it.

He believed that monarchs had a 'Divine Right' to rule. This meant that they were chosen by God who gave them the right to rule. 'They are called gods even by God himself,' he told Parliament.

What James meant was that members should shut up and do what they were told. After all, they would not argue with God. So James thought that anyone who argued with him was a traitor.

But James had a problem. He needed money to run the country. Most of his income came from taxes but there was never enough money. Even Elizabeth had found herself short of cash. James had a wife and family to support – and prices were going up.

To get more money, James had to ask Parliament. But even Elizabeth had found that MPs could be awkward. Controlling taxes was their best weapon. Over the next few years, they were to use it well.

James tried to raise taxes himself, without asking Parliament. In fact, he wanted to do most things without Parliament. He tried to marry his son, Charles, to the King of Spain's sister.

Many members of Parliament were Puritans. Not surprisingly, they were furious. They still thought of Catholic Spain as England's great enemy. They wanted Charles to marry a Protestant – and they wanted James to go to war with Spain. James told the MPs that it was none of their business.

B James I, painted in about 1620. In the background you can see the Banqueting House, still standing in Whitehall today.

1. a) Look at source B. Describe what James I looked like.
   b) Now, describe what sort of person you think he was.
   c) Which of these tasks was easier?
   d) What does this teach you about paintings as evidence?

Members of Parliament wanted more power. So they declared that it was their right to talk about any topic of importance. They wrote down this decision in their journal . James was so angry that he tore the page out of the book.

In 1625, James caught a fever and died. He was buried in Westminster Abbey but no one noted down *where* in Westminster Abbey. It was another 250 years before anyone thought of looking. They found his corpse in the tomb of Henry VII. The first Tudor and the first Stuart were buried together.

How they disagreed

C From the *Works of James I* (1616).
Kings are not only God's lieutenants upon earth and sit upon God's throne, but even by God himself they are called gods.

D James I wrote this to his son Charles:
Learn to know and love God ... [because] he made you a little God, to sit on his Throne, and rule over other men.

E John Selden, a member of Parliament, took a different view:
A king is a thing men have made for their own sakes, for quietness' sake. Just as in a family one man is appointed to buy the meat.

F James I told the Spanish Ambassador in 1614:
The [MPs] give their opinions in a disorderly manner. Nothing is heard but cries, shouts and confusion at their meetings. I am a stranger, and found [Parliament] here when I arrived, so I am obliged to put up with what I cannot get rid of.

G A 16th-century painting of a young golfer. Golf was already popular in Scotland and James himself was interested in it. (His mother Mary played the game.)

When reading sources, historians have to separate facts from opinions. Most sources contain some opinions, even if they are not at first obvious.

2. a) In pairs, study sources C to F. Think carefully. Write down any facts in these sources.
   b) Write down James I's opinion of kings.
   c) Write down John Selden's opinion of kings.
   d) In source D, what is James teaching his son?
   e) Was it possible for the king and John Selden to agree? Explain your answer.

3. a) Still in pairs, read again paragraphs two and three on page 34. Write down any facts you can find.
   b) Explain how you might prove these facts.
   c) Write down any opinions in the two paragraphs. Explain how you decided that they were opinions, rather than facts.

4. a) Look at source A. Design a flag which you think would satisfy both Scotland and England.
   b) Some of you can explain your designs to the class.
   c) Do you think these designs would please both the Scots and the English? Discuss your views.
   d) What can you learn from this exercise?

9 TOWARDS CIVIL WAR

A Charles with his Catholic wife, Queen Henrietta Maria. She never understood Parliament and urged Charles to stand up for his rights. The king himself was just 4ft 7ins (140cms) tall.

> In 1642, England found itself at war. It was not a war with Spain or, indeed, with any other foreign country. England was at war with itself. One group of people fought another. We call this a civil war. These two pages look at what caused this war.

Divine Right

After James's death, the next king was his son, Charles. Like his father, Charles believed in Divine Right. As he was chosen by God, Charles thought Parliament should do what he said. But Parliament had made up its mind to have more control over running the country.

Charles needed money

Prices were rising yet the king's income was not much bigger than that of monarchs of the middle ages. Charles asked Parliament for more money. The members gave him just one seventh of what he wanted so he dismissed them.

Eleven Years Without Parliament

In 1628, Charles called a third Parliament. He was still trying to get money out of them. Instead, they granted him money for just one year. Charles had had enough. He closed Parliament down. For eleven years, he did without it.

Fines and loans

Many people agree that the country was well-run, even without Parliament, but it meant that Charles was very short of cash. He had to bring back all sorts of fines which people had not paid since the middle ages.

Ship Money

The most hated tax of all was Ship Money. The king had the right to collect this tax from people living near the sea. This did not satisfy Charles. He also taxed those living far inland.

One of those who would not pay was a rich gentleman called John Hampden. He was put on trial. The verdict was close: out of twelve judges, seven found him guilty. But many people still thought he was innocent. They blamed the king.

The Bishops' Wars

One of Charles's main advisers was William Laud, the Archbishop of Canterbury. In 1637, he ordered the Scots to use a new prayer book. (Until then, Scottish ministers made up their own prayers.) The Scots were angry and decided to fight the English. That meant Charles needed an army – but soldiers cost money. There was only one way he could get it: he had to call a Parliament.

B In 1637, three Puritans had been punished for attacking the power of bishops. Part of the punishment was having their ears cut off. This cartoon (from 1637) shows Laud at dinner.

The Final Quarrels

In 1640, Parliament met again. This time, they were determined to get their way. The king's chief minister, Strafford, was executed. Charles had to sign the death warrant. He hesitated before he did this but he was frightened that his wife and children might be attacked. So Strafford went to his death. Laud ended up in prison. (He, too, had his head cut off, in 1645.)

Before Parliament gave Charles any money, it gave him a long list of complaints. They called it 'The Grand Remonstrance'. Charles had had enough and decided he would arrest five of the leading MPs. Along with 300 armed men, he marched to the House of Commons.

This painting, made long afterwards, shows the scene inside the House of Commons. The king is on the right.

But the members had been tipped off. When Charles arrived, the five MPs were nowhere to be seen. 'I see,' said Charles, 'all the birds are flown.'

Trying to arrest the MPs was really the last straw for Parliament. In the streets of London, an angry mob gathered and marched towards the palace. Even Charles's home no longer seemed safe.

So he left the capital and headed north to get an army together. The queen sailed for Holland with the crown jewels. Her job was to find the money to pay for an army.

In August 1642, the king raised his flag at Nottingham. It was so huge that it needed 20 men to lift it. Soon afterwards, it was blown down. Was this a bad omen for the king?

D Charles I spent a lot of money on art. This ceiling was painted for the king by Rubens in 1635. It shows James I swapping his earthly crown for a heavenly one.

One thing which historians want to know is *why* the civil war happened. What caused it? Like all events, it had more than one cause. Some of the causes were long-term. These included problems which had existed for many years before war broke out. Others were short-term causes. In other words, they were things which happened just before the war started.

Please work in pairs.
1 a) Divide a sheet of paper into two columns. On one, put the heading *Long-term causes*. On the other, write *Short-term causes*.
b) Find as many causes as you can in the text. Write each in the column you think is correct. The headings will help.
c) Now, look at each picture in turn. For each one, decide whether it suggests a *different* cause. If so, add it to your columns.
d) Look back at pages 34-5. See if you can find even more causes to add to your list.
e) Finally, read these two pages again. Are there any causes which are not mentioned in the headings? If so, add those, too.
f) Look at your list. Decide which cause you think is most important. (You may choose more than one, if you wish.) Note down why you think it is so important.
g) As a class, compare your answers. What does this comparison teach you about the problems of working out why events happen?

10 CIVIL WAR AND AFTER

1500 1525 1550 1575 1600 1625 1650 1675 1700 1725 1750

How the sides lined up. The country gentry were divided while ordinary country folk tended to support whoever their local gentry supported.

So the civil war began. The main issue was: who was to rule the country? Would it be the king or Parliament? However, religion also played a part, as you can see above.

Most people tried to keep out of the war but that didn't stop them being affected by it. At Dunstable, the Royalists raided the town in 1644 and took pot-shots at the minister during a service. At Devizes, they took the lead from the church roofs and turned it into bullets. Wherever you lived, war was not far away.

When the men rode off to fight, the women were left behind to defend their homes. Many showed great bravery. The Countess of Derby was besieged for two years until Royalists came to her help.

In Oxfordshire, Mrs Jones hid her husband, Arthur, in a secret room. When Roundhead soldiers turned up, she calmly offered them wine which was drugged. When they fell asleep, she helped her husband to escape – on one of their horses!

Yet few people actually fought in the war. Each side had an army of only about 70,000 men. Nor did these armies do much fighting. There were just three great battles. However, there were also hundreds of smaller clashes when small groups of gentry went hunting the enemy.

The king's supporters had the best cavalry, yet both sides claimed they had won the Battle of Edgehill (1642). But the summer of 1643 brought many Royalist victories and the Roundheads realised they had to train better cavalry. They gave the job to Oliver Cromwell who organised new troops in East Anglia. They called them *Ironsides*.

In the winter of 1644-5, Parliament went one better. It created a new army, with proper scarlet uniforms, proper training and regular pay – more like a modern army. They called these men *The New Model Army*. This photograph shows people acting out one of the battles.

A

This new army proved how good it was at the Battle of Naseby (1645). The king's army was almost wiped out. Over 1000 were killed; most of the rest were taken prisoner or had simply run away. Charles, too, decided to give up. He surrendered to the Scots.

The Scots gave him to Parliament in return for their pay. Soon afterwards, Charles found himself locked up on the Isle of Wight. Despite this, he did not give up. He plotted to get a Scottish army to invade England. When it did, it was crushed by the New Model Army.

Cromwell was quite clear what should happen next. Charles must be tried and executed. But many MPs did not agree. Cromwell had a solution for that, too. In December 1648, soldiers surrounded Parliament. Anyone who still supported Charles was kept out.

Who won the Battle of Edgehill?

Each side claimed a victory. Sources B and C are primary sources; source D is the opinion of a modern historian.

B A supporter of Parliament wrote this:
On Wednesday Lord Wharton and Mr Strowd came into St Margaret Church. [They] gave a paper to the [preacher] to give God thanks for the victory. 3000 were slain on the King's side and 300 on theirs.

C A supporter of the king wrote this:
On Sunday last I saw the Battle which was the bloodiest I believe the oldest soldiers ever saw. We have utterly [defeated] their horse and slain & chased away so many of their infantry, that the enemy is very weak. The King hath five hundred of their horse alive. Of eighteen hundred not one horse is left them.

D Peter Gaunt: *The Cromwellian Gazetteer* (1987).
The two forces [separated] at nightfall, slept in the field and then marched away on the 24th. Both sides had lost around 700 men apiece and the battle was [in effect] a draw.

E Oliver Cromwell (top left) preaching in church. The figure with him is an angel.

F This propaganda picture from the war shows soldiers committing crimes.

Accounts of events often differ because the writers (or artists) had different viewpoints. Some sources were deliberate propaganda. Historians have to compare sources to find out what really happened.

1. Look at sources E and F. Which side do you think produced each one? Explain how you decided.
2. a) Read sources B, C and D. How do they disagree about the battle? Quote from the sources in your answer.
   b) Suggest reasons why even eye-witnesses might disagree about what happened in a battle.
   c) Suggest reasons why a secondary source about a battle might be more reliable.
   d) Which source proves that at least one side used this battle as propaganda?
3. Look at source A. What research would these people have done to produce this scene?
4. a) While Charles I was in prison, he used this code. Make up a message for the king, using the code.

b) Exchange messages with a partner and try to decode their message.

CHANGE UNDER CROMWELL

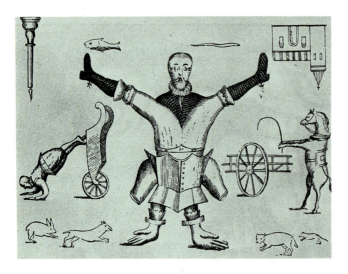

A This cartoon was published in 1642. The artist has shown the world turned upside down.

On 30 January 1649, King Charles I stepped out of his palace in Whitehall onto a scaffold. A jury had found him guilty of various crimes, including treason. That afternoon, at just after 2 o'clock, he lay his head on the block. Two disguised executioners cut it off.

England was now a republic – a country which is not ruled by a king or queen. Instead, Parliament was in control. But the person with real power was Oliver Cromwell, who had become commander-in-chief of the army. This picture of him was painted in about 1649.

The House of Lords was abolished and England was ruled by the House of Commons until 1653. But, when its members argued about having new MPs, Cromwell sent them home. Later that year, he took control as Lord Protector.

Cromwell would have allowed anyone to worship as they wished but others were less tolerant. Most people were given religious freedom but Catholic services were still banned. Protestants could have almost any service they wished, as long as they did not use the Anglican Prayer Book.

During the next five years Cromwell tried all sorts of ways of running the country. But the leading Puritans were enjoying real power for the first time. They intended to use it.

They believed that Sunday was a day of rest. So they only allowed people to walk to and from church. Anyone else out on the roads was fined. Even washing clothes was banned on Sundays.

Puritans were very strict about their religion. They believed in the Devil. One place they thought he was at work was the theatre. So the playhouses were closed down. Even Christmas Day was abolished in 1652.

In 1655, the country was divided into 11 areas, with a major-general in charge of each. Most of them were firm Puritans and very unpopular. They banned cock-fights and bear-baiting; even dancing round a maypole on May Day was stopped. In fact, almost all entertainments disappeared.

When Cromwell died in 1658, one writer said, 'It was the joyfullest funeral I ever saw.' Cromwell's son, Richard, took over, but he had little interest in the job. A new Parliament soon asked Charles I's son to become the new monarch.

Cromwell was dead but his influence has been with us ever since. He allowed Jews to live in England for the first time since 1290. Groups like the Quakers could hold their own services. After 1660, the Church of England tried to crush the new religious groups. It attacked them but it could not destroy them. They have Cromwell to thank for that.

C These fines were recorded in the parish records of St Giles, London.

1652 Mr Huxley and Mr Morris, who were riding out of town in sermon time on a Fast day	65p
1654 Isaac Thomas a barber in Holborn, for trimming a beard on the Lord's day	sum not recorded
1655 A Scotchman drinking at Robert Owne's on the Sabbath (Sunday)	10p
1658 Joseph Piers for refusing to open his doors to have his house searched on the Lord's day	50p

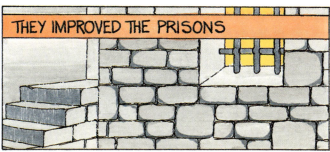

THEY IMPROVED THE PRISONS

THEY TOOK BETTER CARE OF THE MENTALLY ILL

ALL BIRTHS AND DEATHS WERE REGISTERED

Some of the improvements during this period.

D Ann Monsarrat described what happened to weddings in *And The Bride Wore* (1973).

The Puritans did not approve of white wedding dresses; they believed that marriages should be performed with the minimum of fuss and ceremony. For the three years after 1653, the only legal marriage was one performed before a justice of the peace.

In 1656, most marriages returned to the churches but not to the Anglican marriage service. The *Book of Common Prayer* was banned and a new *Directory for Publick Worship* replaced it. Wedding rings were frowned on – 'a circle for the devil to dance in' was how one Puritan put it – but most people continued to use them.

One result is still with us. It was the idea that one should not marry on Sundays. This popular wedding day never became fashionable again.

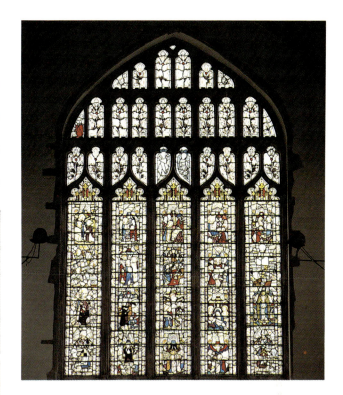

E Puritans preferred plain churches so soldiers destroyed such things as statues and crosses. This 15th-century glass in a Norfolk church only survived because it was taken out and hidden.

The rule of Parliament and Cromwell brought many changes. These were of different kinds: there were religious, political and social changes. Some of them have lasted down to the present day.

1. Explain the meanings of these words: republic, Parliament, Puritan.
2. Look at source A. Write down all the ways in which the artist showed that the world was upside down.
3. a) List all the changes you can find on these two pages.
   b) For each one, write down whether it was religious, political or social.
   c) Which kind of change would have most affected ordinary people? Explain how you decided.
   d) Which of these changes have lasted until modern times?
4. Some pubs were given new names, such as *Adam and Eve*. Choose a suitable name for a pub at this time. Then, design a pub sign for it.
5. a) Suppose a 17th-century Puritan spent a day with *you* this week. What would shock them about (i) your attitude to religion and (ii) how you live?
   b) Does that mean you are wicked? Explain your answer carefully.

11 CHARLES II, THE MERRY MONARCH

1500　1525　1550　1575　1600　1625　1650　1675　1700　1725　1750

On 29 May 1660, Charles I's son returned to London on his 30th birthday. The new king, Charles II, was determined that he would not have *his* head cut off. He had spent the last 11 years wandering around Europe. For much of the time, he was broke.

It was quite a homecoming. The church bells rang throughout Wales; in towns such as Manchester, wine ran from the public fountains. In London, a huge crowd watched as Charles rode through the streets.

A

One person who watched these events was a young government official called Samuel Pepys, shown above. That year, on 1 January, he had started keeping a diary. It was a private diary so he wrote it in shorthand.

That first day, Pepys had had turkey for dinner; his wife Elizabeth had burnt her hand while preparing it. But his diary was more than just an account of his personal life. Pepys knew important people and described the great events of his time.

B For instance, he was there when the king landed at Dover on 25 May 1660. This is what he wrote:
> The Mayor presented him from the town a very rich Bible, which he took, and said it was the thing that he loved above all things in the world... The shouting and the joy expressed by all is past imagination.

Cromwell's body was later dug up and hanged in front of a huge crowd. Afterwards, his head was publicly displayed, stuck on a pole. But Charles II was not looking for revenge. Only a few of those who helped to convict Charles I were executed.

C On 13 October 1660, Pepys saw an execution:
> I went out to Charing Cross to see Major-General Harrison hanged, drawn and quartered. He [looked] as cheerful as any man could in that condition. He was presently cut down, and his head and heart shown to the people. There were great shouts of joy.
>
> Thus it was my chance to see the King beheaded at White Hall, and to see the first blood shed in revenge for the King at Charing Cross.
>
> I went by water home, where I was angry with my wife for her things lying about. [I] kicked the little basket which I bought her in Holland, and broke it, which troubled me after I had done it.

Parliament had ruled the country after the death of Charles I. His son knew he would have to get on with Parliament. Unlike his father, he could not just ignore it.

On the other hand, Parliament was keen to get on with the king. It gave him a regular income of over £1 million pounds a year. However, this wasn't really enough to run the country.

D Charles II was intelligent, witty and easy-going – quite unlike his father. His wife had no children but he had at least 14 by other women, including Nell Gwyn. This painting shows his gardener giving him the first English pineapple.

This one picture sums up how much life changed after 1660. It shows Nell Gwyn, an actress who was one of the king's mistresses. Theatres were reopened after 1660 and actresses appeared on stage for the first time. Also, Nell Gwyn was sometimes painted partly nude. This would have been unthinkable while the Puritans were in power.

E

Charles had promised that people would be allowed to worship as they wished. But he found (as Cromwell had) that Parliament was less tolerant than he was. The Church of England became the country's official religion and the bishops got their jobs back. It has remained so, ever since.

But the Civil War had divided people into those who supported the Church of England and those who did not. Parliament passed a series of acts against the nonconformists – those people who did not *conform* to the Church of England.

Most people had had enough of Puritan ideas and wanted to enjoy themselves. Charles II set a good example of how to go about it. With the king's support, both drama and music made a comeback.

It was a pleasure-loving age. Yet three serious events happened during Charles's reign. One was a war with the Dutch over trade. At one point, Dutch gunfire could be heard in London.

Before that, Pepys had already lived through two other disasters. The first was in 1665, when plague struck the city of London. In 1666, Londoners faced a new danger. Fire.

Three views of King Charles II

F *England and Europe* (a school textbook, 1933).
Charles II was the ablest of the Stuart monarchs. He was charming and witty. He was far cleverer than most of his subjects realized. Charles was selfish and lazy, but he understood his people. He made the monarchy strong again.

G *Marten and Carter's Histories* (1927).
As a ruler, Charles II was easy-going. In religion he was the most tolerant man of all in his Court. But he was a [lazy] man. 'I am more lazy than I ought to be,' he once said. Moreover, he had no deep [beliefs] and his influence on the nation was not good.

H Antonia Fraser: *King Charles II* (1979).
He was not a Merry Monarch. Never has a popular catch-phrase been so [misleading]. The age itself might be merry but [Charles] was marked by [sadness] at the very heart.

Secondary sources often disagree. This may be because the writers hold different opinions or because they have relied on different primary sources.

1 Put these events in the order in which they happened:
a) Cromwell's body dug up;
b) The plague of 1665;
c) The Dutch threatened London;
d) Charles II became King;
e) The Great Fire of London.

2 a) Who wrote sources B and C?
b) When did he write them?
c) Why did he write them?
d) Look at your answers to b) and c). Does this mean these sources are likely to be reliable or not? Give a reason.

3 a) What changes were there after 1660?
b) Which do you think most shocked the Puritans? Explain how you decided.
c) Were these changes caused by politics or religion? Explain carefully.

4 a) Read sources F, G and H. Which one gives the best opinion of Charles II? Give reasons.
b) Which one gives the worst opinion of him? Again, give reasons.
c) How do sources F and G agree with this chapter? Use words from the sources in your answer.
d) Look very carefully. How does source H disagree with this chapter?

THE GREAT FIRE OF LONDON

It was the early hours of Sunday morning, 2 September 1666. Two men were woken up. One was Samuel Pepys. The other was the Lord Mayor of London. The reason was a fire spreading through the city. Each looked and decided it wasn't serious. Each was wrong.

It all started in the king's baker's shop in Pudding Lane. The oven overheated and set the house on fire. The baker and his wife scrambled to safety through an upstairs window, but their maid was frightened of falling to the street below. She stayed where she was and was burned to death.

It had been a hot summer in London. The wooden houses were as dry as they could be. A strong wind from the east caught the flames and carried them through the city. Sparks floated through the air.

By the morning, 300 houses had been destroyed. Now, Pepys was worried. After all, there was no fire brigade. Leather buckets and metal squirts were the only way of putting water on the flames. Fire-hooks could be used to pull down a burning house but no one seemed to be doing this. So Pepys went to see the king.

Charles II sent him to the Lord Mayor with a message: 'Spare no houses but pull down before the fire every way.' The idea was to create a fire-break. This might stop the fire spreading to more houses.

Pepys found the Mayor in despair. People were not obeying him. 'I have been pulling down houses,' he said, 'but the fire overtakes us faster than we can do it.' He was exhausted.

By Monday morning, the heart of the city was ablaze. Terrified Londoners were leaving in panic. Carts were piled high with people's possessions. Ferries took people and their goods across the Thames to safety.

On Wednesday, the Duke of York brought in sailors to blow up houses. Gaps were made to stop the fire spreading. By Thursday, the fire was dying down, although you could still burn your shoes on the red-hot cobbles of the streets. Even some fire-engines had caught fire.

It had all started with an oven in Pudding Lane. It ended at Pie Corner! About 100,000 people lost their homes and nearly 90 churches were destroyed. Perhaps the greatest loss was St Paul's Cathedral. One person wrote, 'London is no more.'

A A contemporary picture of the fire.

B An extract from Samuel Pepys' diary, 2 September:

We saw the fire grow . . . in a most horrid, bloody flame, not like the fine flame of an ordinary fire. We stayed till, it being darkish, we saw the fire as one entire arch of fire from this to the other side of the bridge, and up the hill for above a mile long: it made me weep to see it. The churches, houses and all on fire, and flaming at once; and a horrid noise the flames made, and the cracking of houses at their ruin. So home with a sad heart, and there find everybody [talking] and lamenting the fire.

Alms money which was collected in the said Parish on the Fast Day, being the 10th day of October 1666. towards the Relief of those Persons who have been great Sufferers by the late Sad Fire within the City of London.

C This receipt shows that villagers in Cowfold, Sussex collected about £2.68 for those who suffered from the fire.

What London lacked in 1666. There was no fire brigade or proper police; there was no house insurance or telephones.

D A hand squirt and a leather bucket of the time. The squirt held a gallon (4.5 litres) of water and needed three men to operate it.

We have a number of sources for our knowledge of the Great Fire. There are objects, such as source D and documents, such as source C. There are also written accounts, such as Pepys' diary. The sources a historian uses affect his or her interpretation of events.

1 Which of the sources (A to D) are useful for learning about:
   a) Londoners' feelings about the fire;
   b) Why the fire spread so easily;
   c) What people outside London did?

E In 1671-6, a monument was put up near the bakery where the fire had started. An inscription on it has since been removed. This extract from a 1976 book explains why.

On the North side, the original inscription stated that the Fire was caused 'by the treachery of the [Catholics] . . . to introduce [the Catholic religion] and slavery'. It was [wrongly] believed that the Fire was deliberately started by the Catholics. This inscription was removed when a Catholic, James II, came to the throne.

2 a) What can a historian learn from sources A, C and D? (Give at least three different answers.)
   b) What can you learn from diaries that you cannot learn from pictures and objects?
   c) What were Pepys' feelings about the fire?
   d) How were the people of Cowfold affected?
   e) How useful do you think source A is?

3 a) Read source E. How does this add to your knowledge of Londoners' feelings about the fire?
   b) How does this add to your understanding of the causes of the fire? (Be careful!)

4 a) Please work in pairs. Each of you writes one or two paragraphs about the fire. One of you uses sources A to E only. The other uses only the text on page 44.
   b) Afterwards, compare your accounts. As a group, discuss why they differ.

12 CHRISTOPHER WREN

During the 15th century, Italian artists began to read again the books of the ancient Greeks and Romans. In ancient times, Rome had been the centre of art and culture. Now, people showed a new interest in the ideas of those times.

They called this period 'the Renaissance' because *Renaissance* means *rebirth*. All the ancient knowledge was being born anew. Gradually, these ideas spread across Europe. In the 16th century, English artists, too, copied the ideas of the ancient Romans.

One person who did so was an architect called Christopher Wren. On 11 September 1666, Wren sent King Charles a plan. It showed how London could be rebuilt after the great fire. It included new, wide streets and fine buildings. Out of the ashes, Wren planned a new London.

In the end, it never happened. People who were homeless wanted to build new homes as quickly as possible. Many wanted to gain a little land, if they could. Surveyors staked out new buildings during the daytime; at night, the owners sometimes came and shifted the stakes.

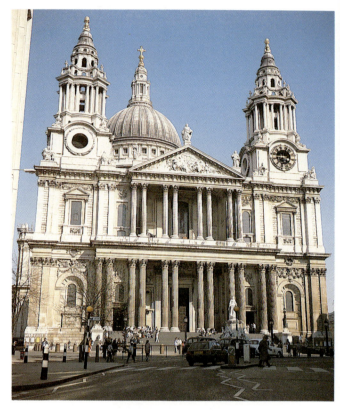

B The new St Paul's Cathedral, built by Sir Christopher Wren from 1675 to 1710.

It would have been expensive to buy land to use for new streets. So Wren's plans were forgotten. Instead, London was rebuilt, using the old street layout of the middle ages. However, Wren was allowed to design many of the new churches. The ideas he used came from the Renaissance.

Wren's most famous church was St Paul's Cathedral. He planned to rebuild it 'after a good Roman manner' and that is what he did. It took 35 years – and he was paid about £4 a week. He was 78 before he watched his son put the last stone on the very highest point of the cathedral.

He had also designed over 50 new churches for which he was paid nothing at all. And he may have helped to design the stone pillar called the Monument. This still stands as a reminder of the great fire, not far from where it started.

Today, visitors still climb the stairs up the column and look out over London. Many of the church spires they see were designed by Wren. So was the dome of St Paul's. That's why Wren's tomb in the cathedral has these words on the side: 'If you seek his monument, look around you'.

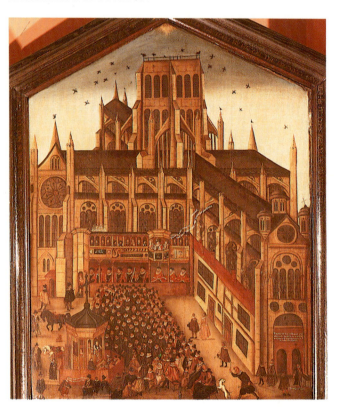

A Old St Paul's Cathedral, as it was before the fire. Its spire had been damaged by lightning in 1561.

C Above: a modern artist's reconstruction of Sir Christopher Wren's plan for the new city. The dome of St Paul's is on the far left; the Monument is in the foreground.

D Below: the same area of London in the 1990s.

There were bound to be changes after the Great Fire. The government made sure that new houses were made of stone or brick, not wood. Some drains were built; there was better collection of rubbish. However, not all the changes brought progress like this.

1 a) Look at sources A and B. How was the new St Paul's different to the old one?
b) *Think* carefully. In what ways was it similar to the old one?
c) What improvements were made to London after the fire?
d) For each one, explain how people benefited from the change.

2 a) Look at sources C and D. How are they different? Write down as many differences as you can.
b) Which of these changes are caused because Wren's plan was not accepted?
c) If London had been built as in source C, how would it benefit these people today: (i) motorists, (ii) pedestrians and (iii) the inhabitants?
d) Are today's traffic jams the fault of 17th-century builders? Explain your answer carefully.

13 SCIENCE

Someone else was busy in the year of the great fire. His name was Isaac Newton. He was a scientist and one of the greatest who ever lived. That year, Newton was busy carrying out experiments with light.

A One of them involved using a prism (a small piece of glass with three sides). He described what happened:
I [got] a glass-Prism, to try the [famous] Phenomena of Colours. Having darkened my chamber, and made a small hole in my window-shuts, to let in a quantity of the Sun's light, I placed my Prism at his entrance, that it might be refracted to the opposite wall.

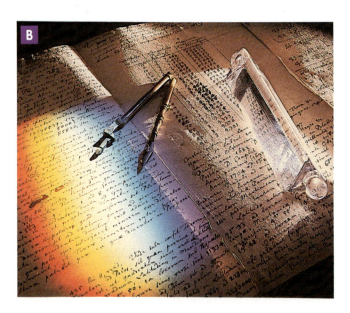

B

This was the result. It was a long band of colours, like a rainbow – red, orange, yellow, green, blue, indigo and violet. This was not new. People had been able to do this for a thousand years. But they had not known why it happened. Newton proved that these colours together make up white light.

Newton should have been studying at Cambridge University at the time. But plague had broken out there in 1665. So Newton had gone home. It was there that he made his greatest discovery. This was the idea that things fall to the ground because a force pulls them down. We call this force *gravity*. Newton was the man who first wrote about it.

It was quite new for scientists to be making experiments like this. Few people had experimented during the middle ages. The Church had taught people that the Bible contained everything they needed to know. However, the Renaissance encouraged people to seek their own answers.

At the time, much science and medicine was sheer guesswork. For instance, most doctors still based their work on the books of a Greek doctor called Galen. They had been written about 1400 years earlier.

One of Galen's ideas was that blood passed from one side of the heart to the other through holes in a thick membrane . In the 16th century, doctors began to have doubts about this theory. For a start, they could not see the holes.

An Englishman, William Harvey, carried out experiments. He came to believe that the heart *pumped* blood through the body. It was the most important medical discovery of the century.

C Harvey explains his ideas to Charles I in this painting made in the 19th century.

D Harvey wrote down his ideas in his notebook, probably in about 1627 or 1628.

It is clear from the heart's structure that the blood passes continually through the lungs to the aorta , as if it were driven by two water-pumps. The blood must move in a constant circle and is driven by the heart's power.

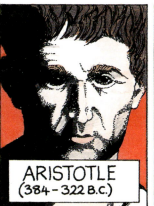

New, and better, telescopes created a lot of interest in science. All sorts of people spent their spare time trying to make their own discoveries.

It was natural that these scientists would want to meet and talk about their ideas. So, starting in 1645, a group of them met each week in London. They also showed each other new experiments.

They were supported by King Charles II. In 1662, he let them call themselves The Royal Society. A few years later, he founded an observatory at Greenwich.

Despite the king's support, some people did not accept these new ideas. Harvey himself admitted that he lost patients after he published his book in 1628. People said he was 'crack-brained'. It was another 20 years before Europe's universities supported his views.

1. What did these people discover: (a) Newton, (b) Harvey and (c) Galileo?
2. Look at the following statements. Write out any which you think are correct and explain why the others are wrong.
   (i) Harvey had to experiment before learning how the heart worked.
   (ii) The Renaissance encouraged people to experiment.
   (iii) The lens had to be invented before the telescope.
   (iv) The telescope had to be invented before people could study the sky in detail.
   (v) Newton had to discover gravity before people could stand on the earth.
   (vi) Plague had to break out at Cambridge before Newton could experiment.

14 SUPERSTITION AND WITCHCRAFT

People of the 16th and 17th centuries were very superstitious. Queen Elizabeth's coronation date was only chosen after the stars had been studied. In 1666, before the Great Fire, people had seen comets in the sky. They were a bad omen.

Although scientists were carrying out experiments, superstition did not die overnight. Even Newton was interested in alchemy. This involved trying to turn cheap metals into gold.

People then did not have the medical knowledge we now do. They could not understand how a person could suddenly drop down dead – or why the crop was so bad one year. They looked for a reason. The answer, they often decided, was that a witch was at work.

The first law against witches was passed in 1542. During the 17th century, hundreds of witches were executed. Most were poor; many were old women. The Church believed that women were more likely to become witches because 'they could reach the depths of evil'. The picture shows a typical victim.

A This medieval French painting shows a witches' meeting.

USUALLY AN OLD PERSON, LIVING ALONE.

THEY OFTEN TALKED TO THEMSELVES.

A 'FAMILIAR' (AN ANIMAL WHICH WAS REALLY THE DEVIL IN DISGUISE)

Lawyers wrote books which told people how to spot a witch. One easy way was to look for an unusual spot on the person's body. This was a sign of the devil. Seeing the witch feed a familiar was another sign.

William Harvey was one doctor who was often called on to give his opinion. One one occasion, he visited an old woman in Newmarket. People round about were convinced she was a witch. Dr Harvey pretended to be a wizard and asked to see her familiar.

She brought out a toad and gave it some milk. Dr Harvey then got the old woman out of the house, caught the toad and cut it up. He examined it carefully and decided it was just an ordinary toad. The old woman had tamed it.

People accused of being witches were often kept awake night after night. Judges claimed it was done to find out if they were visited by their familiars. Of course, this weakened old people. They were more likely to plead guilty.

If there was any doubt, two tests could be used. One involved sticking a large pin in the person. If they felt no pain, it was a sign that the devil had put a mark on them.

The better-known way was 'swimming'. First, a pond or river was blessed by a vicar. Then, the 'witch' was tied up and lowered into the water. If the person floated, it was sign that the 'holy' water refused to receive him or her.

A person who sank was innocent. In theory, he or she was then hauled out. But often the judges wanted to be sure. So they left the person in the water just a little longer. For an old person, it might be just enough to kill them.

Over 100,000 people were put to death for witchcraft in Europe during the 16th and 17th centuries. Many were burned alive, as in Scotland. Yet attitudes were slowly changing. The last English trial was in 1712; in Scotland, it was ten years later. Witchcraft ceased to be a crime in 1736.

B Inside jars like these, people kept nail-clippings and other odds and ends. They thought a witch would be attracted to them and get trapped in the jar.

C Every region had its charms. This one was used in Cambridgeshire.
Make a black cat spit on mutton fat
Then rub it inside a horse's hat.
Scrape it off within a week
Then go outside a toad to seek
And make it sweat into a pot.
With wooden spoon mix the lot,
And you will have a healing balm
To keep the body free from harm.

D This remedy was noted by Edward Topsell in *The Historie of Serpents* (1608).
The eyes of dragons, kept till they be stale and afterwards beat into an ointment, keep anyone that uses it from the terror of night visions.

E These poems were written by Robert Herrick (1591-1674).
Bring the holy crust of Bread,
Lay it underneath the head;
'Tis a certain Charm to keep
Hags away, while children sleep.

Let the superstitious wife
Near the child's heart lay a knife:
Point be up and Haft be down;
(While she gossips in the town)
This 'mongst other mystick charms,
Keeps the sleeping child from harms.

F George Gifford: *A dialogue concerning witches and witchcraftes* (1593).
There be two or three in our town which I like not, but especially an old woman. I have been careful to please her and to give her one thing or another; and yet methinks she frowns at me now and then. And I had a hog which ate his meat with his fellows and was very well [we thought] overnight, and in the morning he was stark dead. My wife hath had five or six hens dead. Some of my neighbours wish me to burn something alive, as a hen or a hog. Others will me to seek help at the hands of some cunning man, before I have any further harm.

People's ideas are limited by the times in which they live. People in the 16th and 17th centuries did not have the medical and scientific knowledge that we do. However, in any age, there will always be some people (such as Dr Harvey) who disagree with the general view.

1 a) Work as a class. Imagine that a male villager has suddenly dropped down dead. One half of you should write down why a 17th-century person might have thought that the man was bewitched. The other half writes down the explanations which we might give today.
b) When you have done this, the 'modern' person must try to persuade the 17th-century person that the man was not bewitched.
c) What does this teach you about how attitudes change?

2 Look at the drawing of the witch on page 50.
a) Why might this person talk to herself?
b) What might a 17th-century person have thought she was doing?
c) Why might such a person keep an animal?
d) What would we call animals such as this today?

3 a) Read source F. Does this man think his animals are bewitched? Explain your answer.
b) What two actions have been suggested to him?
c) What would a modern farmer do about what happened?
d) Why would a 17th-century farmer not do this?
e) How does this source help you understand why people of the time believed in witches?

15   1688: REVOLUTION

A This painting shows William and Mary on the throne. William is trampling on the French Catholic king.

In 1685, Charles II lay dying. The doctors put hot plasters of pitch and pigeon dung on his body; they blew sneezing powders up his nostrils to clear his head. Neither was successful. Charles had been a popular king and had made the monarch a powerful person once more. However, he had no children so his brother James became the new king.

Charles had been careful not to upset people about religion. James, who was a Catholic, did not bother. Like his father, Charles I, he believed in the Divine Right of Kings.

James had not been king long before there was a rebellion. It was led by the Duke of Monmouth, one of Charles II's many illegitimate children.

James's army soon defeated the rebels and Monmouth was executed. But the rebellion gave James an excuse to increase his army. Over the next three years, Catholics were given powerful jobs. And, like his father, James ruled without Parliament.

People were unhappy about this but not desperately worried. They knew that James could not live forever – and he had no sons. When he died, the next monarch would be his daughter, Mary. She was a Protestant. So was her husband, the Dutch Prince, William of Orange. People thought that the Catholic problem was only temporary.

In June 1688, they found they were wrong. After 15 childless years, James's wife at last gave birth to a son. People feared he would be brought up as a Catholic. If so, they could no longer look forward to a Protestant monarch.

A number of important Protestants decided that the time had come for James to go. A messenger slipped out of the country and sailed for Holland. His letter asked William of Orange to gather an army and sail for England.

On 5 November, William landed in Devon with about 15,000 soldiers. Many people deserted James. They included Lord Churchill, the leader of James's army.

In the end, James set sail for France. He was received by the French king in the royal palace of Versailles. 'When you listen to him,' said a French courtier, 'you realise why he is here.' And there he stayed. He lived in exile until his death in 1701.

Meanwhile, William insisted that he would only stay in England if he were made king. So Parliament made William and Mary joint monarchs. For the first and only time, England had both a king and a queen to rule the country.

B This card comes from a pack which celebrated the revolution. It shows Catholic priests praising God for the arrival of French troops. The event shown did not happen.

C This Dutch engraving shows the 1688 Revolution.

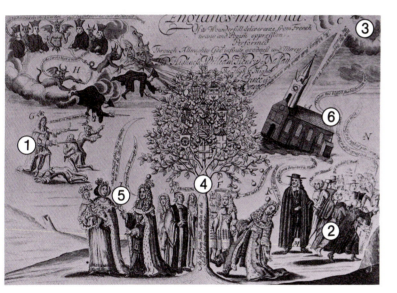

E This contemporary Dutch print shows William of Orange saving England and Europe from various horrors.

D This card comes from the same pack as source B. There were rumours that Catholic priests were intending to torture Protestants. This scene shows an attack on a Catholic chapel in London.

The sources on these two pages are all propaganda. Despite that, they can still provide useful information. For instance, they show what some people at the time were thinking.

1 Put these events in the order they happened:
a) Monmouth's rebellion; b) James sailed to France; c) the death of Charles II; d) the arrival of Prince William.

2 a) Look at source E. Decide what you can see at the numbered places from this list: The Church of England, nearly overturned; James II and his wife; the French king killing his people; Catholics fleeing; God's intervention; the tree (a symbol of Prince William of Orange).
b) Why do you think the artist has included God in this picture?
c) Do you think this artist supported the Catholics or Protestants? Give reasons.

3 a) Look at source C. Decide whom you can see at the four numbered places from this list: William of Orange; James II; Britannia; Mary.
b) Do you think the artist supported William or James? Give reasons for your decision.
c) Nobody died during the event. Why, then, should you be cautious about this source?

4 a) Why were playing cards a good way of spreading propaganda?
b) What did the artists of the five sources want Protestants to feel about (i) Prince William, (ii) Catholic priests and (iii) the French?

5 Which picture do you think makes the best propaganda? Explain how you decided.

16 PARLIAMENT IN CONTROL

1500 1525 1550 1575 1600 1625 1650 1675 1700 1725 1750

A King William III and Queen Mary II.

The year 1688 marked a turning-point in British history. The struggle between Parliament and monarch was over and Parliament had won. After all, Parliament *invited* William and Mary to become king and queen. Never again would monarchs claim they had a 'divine right' to rule.

Parliament also decided who should be the next monarch when they died. If they had no children, the next ruler would be Mary's sister, Anne. Never again would there be a Catholic king of England.

In fact, over the next years, Parliament made sure that future monarchs would do as they were told. It began with the Bill of Rights which Parliament passed in 1689.

There was another problem to settle. Charles II had been able to rule the country without calling a Parliament for 11 years. Parliament wanted to make sure this could never happen again. So it passed the Triennial Act. ('Tri' means 'three'.)

Of course, William and Mary were still more powerful than the British monarch today. But Parliament had one more plan for keeping them under control. It only gave them enough money to rule for one year at a time. That meant Parliament would have to be called regularly – or the monarch would have no money.

Why is all this so important?

The reason is that England was the first major country to bring its monarch under control. It was the first country to elect a Parliament which had real power.

B A century later, there was a revolution in France. As this painting shows, it was a far more bloody event than the English one.

In the meantime, there had been another change. In the 1670s, members of Parliament had begun to form themselves into parties. There were two of them. The Tories , by and large, had supported King James II. The Whigs had wanted to stop James becoming king. In time, they grew into the Conservative and Liberal parties.

C The Toleration Act of 1689 allowed Puritans to worship as they wished. This was a Quaker meeting-house in London.

It seemed as if Parliament had settled the problem of who should rule England. Although William and Mary had no children, Anne was pregnant 17 times. Sadly, all her children died. (Anne thought God was punishing her for deserting her father.)

So, in 1701, Parliament made a new decision. The next monarch would be Anne's closest Protestant relative. When she died in 1714, this person was George, the ruler of Hanover. This was a German state, about the size of Wales.

George I spoke no English and never bothered to learn any. As a result, he rarely attended Cabinet meetings. In his absence, someone had to organise the government's business in the House of Commons.

The man who did this was Robert Walpole, a rich Norfolk landowner. In time, he gained so much power that people nicknamed him *Prime Minister*. Walpole himself did not like the title much – but the name stuck.

It was Walpole who brought the news of King George I's death to his son, the new King George II. 'Dat is vun beeg lie,' said George II. (He *did* speak English, but with a German accent.) He was more interested in Hanover than in England so Parliament's powers increased. Sometimes, Parliament even chose the king's ministers for him.

George II was not the first monarch to complain about 'that damn'd House of Commons'. Elizabeth I had argued with MPs; James I had wanted to get rid of them. But those days were now long past. The Hanoverian kings could not rule without Parliament – but Parliament had shown it could rule without kings.

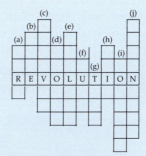

1 Copy out the grid above, then fill in the spaces, using these clues:
a) She became queen in 1689.
b) She became queen in 1702.
c) A German state.
d) He became king in 1714.
e) Queen Mary's husband.
f) What a king or queen does.
g) An opponent of the Whigs.
h) An opponent of the Tories.
i) A word meaning 'king or queen'.
j) This Act was passed in 1694.

2 Look at the list of laws below. For each one, write down (i) what it stopped the monarch from doing and (ii) why this was important.
a) Only Parliament could make laws.
b) Parliament had to agree to all taxes.
c) The monarch could not raise an army without Parliament's agreement.
d) No Parliament could last more than three years.
e) The monarch was only allowed money for one year at a time.

The revolution created a balance between the powers of the King and the powers of Parliament.

17 IRELAND

Very little of Ireland was really controlled by England in 1500. The Norman barons who had settled in Ireland were now as Irish as their neighbours. The last thing they wanted was to be ruled by an English monarch.

The Tudors tried to bring Ireland under the control of the Church of England. But the Irish never really became Protestant and the Catholic religion made a comeback. More than once, the Irish rebelled. Each time, the leaders lost their land, which was given to Protestants.

English monarchs were afraid that the French or Spanish might invade England through Ireland. So James I gave land in Ulster to Scottish Protestants. He hoped that these colonists would keep the Irish under control. By 1640, over 30,000 Scots and English had gone to live in Ireland.

But it was like putting a match to gunpowder. The colonists looked down on the Irish; in return, the Irish hated them. In 1641, the situation exploded in war. The Irish killed huge numbers of settlers; many more died of cold or hunger.

B On 12 July each year, Protestants in Northern Ireland still march to celebrate William's victory over the Catholics.

When Charles I was executed, the Irish proclaimed his son as their king. Cromwell decided the time had come to sort out Ireland once and for all. What followed is still remembered by the Irish with great bitterness. In Drogheda, over 2000 people died when Cromwell took the town. A similar number died in Wexford.

Cromwell believed that it was God's will that he should kill the Irish. 'Blood and ruin shall befall them,' he wrote. At first, any Catholic priest he caught was instantly killed. Later, he sent them to a special camp on a Scottish island.

When it was over, a third of the people of Ireland were dead. Two-thirds of the land was owned by English Protestants. Cromwell had set out to destroy Irish resistance. Instead, he created deep hatred. To many Catholics, he is still known as 'the curse of Ireland'.

When James II tried to get his throne back in 1689, Ireland was the obvious place to start. In 1690, he besieged the town of Londonderry for 15 weeks. The inhabitants were forced to eat rats and mice but they did not give in. Meanwhile, William III had arrived and James's army was defeated at the Battle of the Boyne. The rebellion was over but the seeds of future hatred had been sown.

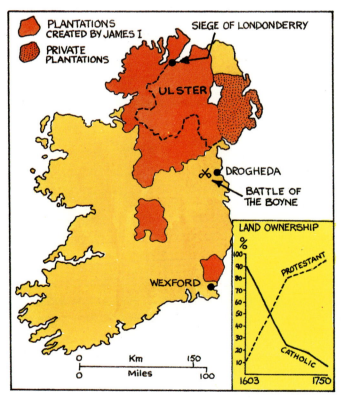

A Map of Ireland, showing where the colonists lived. Ireland became divided between rich Protestants who owned the land – and poor Catholics who did not.

C Oliver Cromwell described the storm of Drogheda on 10 and 11 September, 1649. This letter was written in Dublin on 17 September.

In the heat of action, I forbade [our soldiers] to spare any that were in arms in the Town: and, I think, that night they put to the sword about 2000 men. [Various] officers and soldiers fled into the other part of the Town, where [some took over three strongholds]. These refused to yield.

I ordered the steeple of St Peter's Church to be fired. One of them was heard to say in the midst of the flames: 'God damn me, God confound me; I burn, I burn'.

The next day, from one of the Towers, they killed and wounded some of our men. When they submitted, their officers were knocked on the head. Every tenth man of the soldiers killed; and the rest shipped for the Barbadoes.

I [believe] that this is a righteous judgement of God upon these barbarous wretches, who have [soaked] their hands in so much innocent blood; and that it will prevent the [shedding] of blood for the future.

D Another version of events at Drogheda and Wexford is given in *Ireland's Story* by Désirée Edwards-Rees (1967).

A few years later an English writer, Anthony à Wood, described the scene at Drogheda that his brother Thomas had witnessed. According to Thomas à Wood, when the people took refuge in the churches Cromwell's soldiers pursued them up the towers, holding the children before them as shields. After which, they went down into the vaults to slaughter the women hidden there.

The Bishop of Ferns wrote of Wexford, describing how the priests had either died at their altars or been [whipped], tortured and hanged. 'There was scarcely a house that was not defiled with [death] and full of wailing,' he wrote.

The roots of many modern problems lie in the past. Politicians sometimes think their solution solves a problem. Often, it creates a new one. This is partly because people do not all take the same view of events.

1. a) Did English monarchs think Ireland was a problem? Explain your answer.
   b) Do you think the Irish thought Ireland was a problem? Give reasons.
   c) Compare your answers to a) and b). If they are different, explain why they should be different.
2. a) How did James I and Cromwell deal with Ireland?
   b) How do you think the Irish felt about each of these 'solutions'? Give reasons.
   c) Think carefully. Which one do you think caused the most lasting hatred and why?
3. a) Read sources C and D. Why does source C think killing was the right solution?
   b) What does he hope for the future?
   c) Has he been right? Give reasons.
   d) Does this mean Cromwell's actions at Drogheda were wrong? Explain your answer.
4. a) Work in pairs. One of you is Irish; one is English. Each of you should write down your *feelings* about Cromwell's actions in Ireland. As a class, put these together. Look at the differences.
   b) What consequences do you think these differences would have for Irish history?

In the years after the Battle of the Boyne, the English Parliament passed a number of laws against Catholics. These pictures show how they affected Catholics' lives.

CATHOLICS COULD NOT... ...HAVE CATHOLIC SCHOOLS

...HOLD GOVERNMENT JOBS

...BE AN M.P. OR VOTE IN ELECTIONS

...BE A LAWYER OR A SOLDIER

WEAR A SWORD (THE MARK OF A GENTLEMAN)

OR OWN A HORSE WORTH MORE THAN £5

18 A UNITED KINGDOM...

Between 1500 and 1750, both Wales and Scotland lost their independence. Henry VIII took away Wales's freedom. In 1536 and 1543, Wales was divided into 13 counties which sent MPs to the Parliament at Westminster.

This was a heavy blow to Welsh culture. English law replaced Welsh law. More important, Parliament discussed matters in English. Welsh gentlemen now looked on Welsh as a less important language. All Welsh officials were made to speak English.

The rich Welsh landowners even began to behave as if they were English. They married into English families; their children went to English public schools. The great days of famous Welsh leaders, like Llywelyn, seemed long past.

Yet help for the Welsh language was at hand. As England became Protestant, so did Wales, and this new religion helped keep the Welsh language alive. A Welsh prayer book was published in 1567.

In the next century, many nonconformists spoke Welsh and passed on Welsh culture to their children. Fewer than 500,000 people lived in Wales, even in 1701. Most of them were very poor but their rich culture survived.

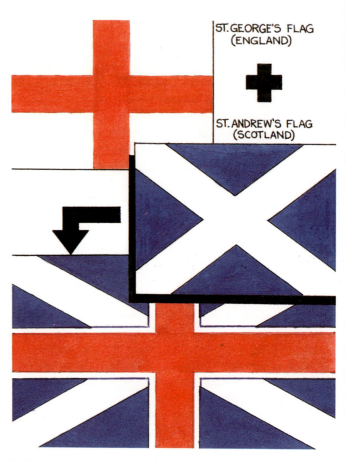

B The symbol of unity from 1606 onwards. When James VI of Scotland also became James I of England, this flag was created. It was still being used in 1750.

In Scotland, the year 1603 was a turning-point. Before he left for England, King James VI told the Scots he would come back to them every third year; in fact, he only once visited his homeland again.

In effect, the Scots were treated as foreigners. Scottish merchants had to pay duties on goods they brought into England. The Scots were not allowed to trade with England's growing empire and the English stopped them from winning their own empire. The English did not want the competition.

The ill-feeling came to a head when the English Parliament decided who should reign after Queen Anne. The Scots were not consulted; the Scottish Parliament said it would choose its own king. The English were worried they would choose a Catholic.

A The title page of the Bible in Welsh, introduced in 1588. The Bible was not translated into the ancient Scottish language of Gaelic.

If that happened, the English would have Catholic rulers on two sides – in France and Scotland. There was a risk that the French might invade England through Scotland.

The English did not want war. But nor did the Scots. They would probably have lost; they would certainly have been ruined. Uniting the two countries seemed to be the best solution.

Plenty of people on both sides did not like the idea. But, in 1707, Scottish MPs voted to end their separate Parliament. Bribes had helped some Scottish MPs to make up their minds.

Scotland at least won a better deal than Wales had done. It lost its Parliament but it kept many other things. Even today, Scotland has its own system of law and religion. It also kept its own school system – set up nearly 200 years before England made every child attend school.

On 1 May 1707, the Act of Union came into effect. In London, Queen Anne went to St Paul's Cathedral to thank God. In Edinburgh, church bells rang out the tune, 'Why should I be sad on my wedding day?'

Others were not so sure that union was a good thing for Scotland. The month before, 31 whales had been found dead on Kirkcaldie sands. It was, said local people, a bad omen: nothing good would come of the union.

For or against union?

C *Modern History*, published by BBC TV (1959).
England, though [a] much larger and wealthier country, has never attempted to deprive Scotland of the privileges promised to her in the 1707 Act of Union. History contains no other example of such [patience] by a great power towards a lesser.

D This verse was carved on the tombstone of Margaret Scott in a Scottish churchyard. It claims she died in 1738, aged 125.
An end of Stuart's race I saw: nay, more!
My native country sold for England's ore.
Such   desolations   in my life have been,
I have an end of all perfection seen.

E L E Snellgrove: *The Early Modern Age* (1972).
[A] flow of educated men and women took the road south, giving their talents and skill for the benefit of Britain. Britain's empire-builders also gained from the thousands of Scots who first helped to conquer and then people the new colonies.

F G M Trevelyan: *Illustrated English Social History* (1944).
The progress of Scotland [from 1751-1800] was not only very rapid but very much in the right direction. Scotland in 1800 was a better place than Scotland in 1700.

Who a person is will affect his or her opinions of events. Scottish people viewed union differently to the English. However, not all Scots took the same view.

1 By now, you should know the following words:
(a) culture; (b) Protestant; (c) Parliament and (d) nonconformist. Write a sentence to explain each of them.
2 Explain the links between the following:
a) Henry VIII, the Reformation and the Welsh language.
b) James II, the 1688 revolution, the Catholic religion and the Act of Union.
3 a) Which Scots benefited from union with England?
b) Which Scots might have been against union? Explain your answer.
c) Why did English people want the union?
d) Which English people might have been against it?
e) Look at sources C, D, E and F. Which do you think was written by a Scot? Explain how you decided.
f) Write down what you think a Scot would think about the other sources.
g) What, therefore, do you need to know about sources before you rely on them?

Many Scots had continued to support James II. There were two attempts to put his   descendants   back on the throne. The second, in 1745, involved James's grandson, Charles Edward Stuart, better known as Bonnie Prince Charlie. When it failed, he fled to France, disguised as a woman.

...WITH REGIONAL DIFFERENCES

A This style of Tudor building was common in Cheshire and Lancashire. This is Speke Hall, near Liverpool.

England, Scotland and Wales were now united. But that did not mean that everyone lived in the same way. There were far greater differences between different regions then than there are today.

For a start, people in each area spoke their own kind of English. A gentleman in Cornwall sounded more like a Cornish labourer than like a gentleman from Norfolk. Each spoke the dialect of his home county.

Probably 25 per cent of English people lived in the north; the south had both more people and more money. However, only a few people in the south were well-off. For instance, about 20 per cent of Devon needed help from the Poor Rates by 1700. Wages varied greatly from one area to another.

So did costume. Each part of England, Scotland and Wales had its own local costume. This photograph was taken in Dyfed long after 1750. It shows an old woman wearing the traditional Welsh costume.

B

C Celia Fiennes found other local costumes on journeys she made in 1698.

You meet all sorts of country women wrapped up in mantles called West Country rockets, a large mantle, and a deep fringe at the lower end. In summer they are all in white garments of this sort, in the winter they are in red ones. They never go out without them. This is the fashion in Somerset and Devonshire and Cornwall.

The Welsh woman is sitting in front of her one-roomed cottage. The window is at the bedroom end of the room. Parts of England were equally poor. In Staffordshire, labourers were still living in houses made of turf in 1680 – and they had no windows at all. Yet this was some years after new buildings in London were being built of stone or brick.

Even what you ate depended partly on where you lived. Bread tasted differently in different areas, according to the corn used. Each region had its own local dishes. These were a few of them.

D The West Country was also famous for another kind of pudding which Celia Fiennes tasted.

My landlady [in Cornwall] brought me one of the West Country tarts; this was the first I met with. It's an apple pie with a custard all on the top. They scald their cream and milk in most parts of those [counties] and so it's a sort of clouted cream, with a little sugar, and put on the top of the apple pie.

I was much pleased with my supper tho' not with the custom of the [area] which is smoking. Men, women and children have pipes of tobacco in their mouths and sit round the fire smoking.

Mostly, people had to make their own entertainment and many local customs developed as a way of having a good time. In the countryside of Wales, men dressed up in a horse's head at Christmas or New Year and visited people's houses. In Scotland, they even went to school on Christmas Day. (They still did in remote parts, early in the 20th century.)

Sport was another way in which areas differed. Some sports, such as football and cock-fighting, were popular everywhere. Others were more local. Golf was popular in Scotland in the 16th century. When James VI became King James I of England, the game came south. In Devon and Cornwall, wrestling was a popular men's pastime.

Wherever you went, you would have found people celebrating traditional events. On May Day, most villages had a maypole, except when the Puritans were in control. Other days, such as Midsummer Day, were also marked by processions and dancing.

E This Midsummer custom took place in Salisbury in 1570. (It may help to read this source aloud.)

May 24th, 1570: Gregory Clark dyd promisse duringe the hole tyme of fyve yeares to fynde and sett goinge for the pageant of Mydsomer feaste, the gyant, the thre black boyes, the bearer of the gyant, and one person to playe the divells part, at [his own expense].

The sayd Gregory . . . shall receyve yerelie [50p] of good and lawfull money of England.

G Two ancient sports which have survived to the present day. Above: tossing the caber is still played in Scotland. Below: less well-known is this game of bullets, played each year in Armagh, Northern Ireland. Each contestant throws an iron ball along a country road. The aim is to go two miles with the least throws. Originally, they used cannon balls!

F This is how the Salisbury giant looks today in the local museum.

1 This question is about why changes have happened. Why do you think:
a) local costumes are rarely worn nowadays?
b) we can all eat foods which come from many parts of the country?
c) most modern houses look much the same, wherever they are?
d) most sports are played throughout the country?

2 Choose any one of the customs or sports mentioned on these two pages. Make up a poster to advertise this event sometime between 1500 and 1750. If you include costumes, make sure they are accurate. Spell any words as they sound.

19 CHANGE AND CONTINUITY

1500　1525　1550　1575　1600　1625　1650　1675　1700　1725　1750

We are used to change these days but people in the 1500s were not. Of course, they were happy to wear new fashions, if they could afford them. They might even smoke the tobacco which traders had brought back from the Caribbean. And there were all sorts of little changes which people noticed.

A William Harrison mentioned some of them in *Description of England* (1587). This is a summary.

There are old men dwelling in my village who have noticed things much changed in England in their lifetimes.
1 Many chimneys have been built. When they were young, there were no more than two or three in many towns.
2 People used to sleep on straw beds, on rough mats covered only with a sheet. They put a log under their heads. Now, they have a feather bed and pillows. Pillows were once used only for women having a baby.
3 Wooden plates have been replaced by pewter ones. People use silver or tin spoons instead of wooden ones.

However, there was one kind of change which people in 1500 thought was wrong. This was changing your position in society. God, they believed, had worked out an order for the world. They did not understand why he had done it, but it existed.

As God had placed the queen at the top, then the queen had to be obeyed. Everyone else had their place; each looked down on those below them.

By the 17th century, attitudes were changing. The kings might still believe in their 'divine right' but many MPs did not. They were no longer prepared just to obey the monarch. By 1750, Parliament had challenged for power and had won.

In 1709, the writer Daniel Defoe divided the population of England into these six groups:
- The great, who live lavishly
- The rich, who have everything they need
- The middle sort, who live well
- The country people, who live neither well nor badly
- The poor, whose life is hard
- The miserable, who live in poverty

Fashions came and went. These pictures show a Puritan couple in about 1650 and another couple a century later.

B Animals, too, suffered, but few people gave it much thought. Cock-fighting remained popular until it was banned in Britain in the 19th century. This modern photograph was taken in France.

Defoe's groups are not so very different from the groups in the drawing on page 15. But many people no longer believed that God had given them a position in life which could never change. Why couldn't a labourer go on to something better?

C Other animals which suffered were whales in the Bay of Biscay. The fashion for ladies' corsets almost wiped them out by the 17th century. The whale boats moved on to Greenland.

Many did. Labourers saved up to buy land; merchants became rich and were given titles; even ordinary people could become people of importance. Of course, in 1750, there were still lords and labourers. But people no longer believed that someone born a labourer had to die as one.

The new attitude brought changes in the way people dressed. In Tudor times, people's clothes showed their position in the world. Lords and ladies wore heavy clothing, with lots of velvet and silk. In 1561, one Exeter boy was fined for wearing a ruff and a silk hat. Those clothes were only for the rich. By 1750, people were wearing whatever they could afford.

However, by 1750, there were still millions of poor people. They were poor in a way we cannot imagine in Britain today. Parents struggled to raise large families on very low incomes. One typical couple was Mr and Mrs Arkwright who lived at Preston in Lancashire.

On 23 December 1732, Mrs Arkwright gave birth to her thirteenth child. They called him Richard. Round about 1750, Richard set himself up as a barber in Bolton.

Two hundred years earlier, that might have been the end of the story. But life was very different in 1750, compared with 1500. Business and industry offered great opportunities to a young man.

When Richard died in 1792, he was worth about £500,000 — a millionaire, by the standards of those days. He had become *Sir* Richard Arkwright, a famous figure in the land. How did he do it? That is something you will have to wait until next year to find out!

---

1 a) Write down each of the changes mentioned in this chapter.
   b) What were the results of each change? (If it does not say, work it out.)
   c) Which things did not change during this period?

2 a) Look at source B. Why do you think attitudes to cock-fighting did not change?
   b) Why, then, do most people nowadays think this sport is cruel?
   c) Look at source C. Why did the whale boats have to change their hunting-ground?

3 Look at these five statements. Decide which you think is an example of progress by 1750 and explain how you made up your mind.
   a) Monarchs no longer ruled by divine right.
   b) Whale boats moved to a new hunting-ground.
   c) Men stopped wearing hats indoors.
   d) People who were well-off could wear whatever they liked.
   e) Poor people wore what they could afford.

GLOSSARY

alchemy – process of changing cheap metals into gold
ancestor – person from whom you are descended
Anglican – of the Church of England
aorta – main artery which carries blood from the left side of the heart
apprentice – person who is learning a craft or trade
arable – growing crops
balm – something which soothes
barbarous – savagely cruel
besieged – surrounded, in an attempt to capture
Cabinet – group of ministers which runs the country
Cardinal – senior official of the Roman Catholic Church
cavalry – soldiers who fight on horseback
chemise – loose underclothing, like a shirt
chide – blame
colonist – person who lives in a colony; settler
contemporary – made at the time
courtier – person who is often present where the monarch lives
cudgel – club
culture – arts and customs of a country at a particular time
descendant – person who comes afterwards, such as a grandchild
desolation – sadness
dialect – way of speaking in a certain area
Divine Right – right to rule, given by God
dole – something given to the poor
doublet – man's close-fitting jacket
Drogheda – you pronounce this: Droy-a-duh
duties – taxes
empire – a number of countries ruled by another country
engraving – carving in wood or metal
galleass – large ship with one deck
galleon – large ship with many decks
haft – handle of a knife
heir – person who will become the next monarch
heretic – person who believes something different to what the Church wants them to believe
illegitimate – person whose parents were not married when he or she was born
infantry – soldiers who fight on foot
inhabitant – person who lives in a particular place
inscription – something cut in stone or metal

interpretation – explanation
inventory – list
journal – daily account, such as a diary
jousting – fighting with lances on horseback
lease – right to use property by paying rent for it
lieutenant – person who acts for a superior
mantle – loose cloak without sleeves
membrane – soft skin
mercer – dealer in cloth
monarch – king or queen. A country ruled by a king or queen is called a monarchy
morals – behaviour
MP – Member of Parliament
nonconformist – Protestant who is not a member of the Church of England
pewter – mixture of tin with other metals
phenomena – events that can be seen
playwright – person who writes plays
Pope – head of the Catholic Church
Privy – private
proclaimed – announced
progress – journey
propaganda – attempts to persuade people to believe something
Protestant – person who protested against the beliefs of the Catholic Church
purify – make pure; cleanse
refracted – bent
relics – things belonging to a holy person
remonstrance – strong protest
revolution – complete change in government
rode – crucifix (the modern spelling is *rood*)
salvation – saving
scald – heat, almost to boiling
shorthand – method of fast writing, using signs instead of letters
slain – killed
Stuart – family name of James I and his relations
Tories – rude nickname for political party. It meant *Scottish robbers*
traitor – person who betrays their monarch or country
treason – crime against the king or country
Tudor – family name of Henry VII and his descendants
Whigs – rude nickname for political party. It meant *Irish robbers*